Y0-BDY-046

The Twenty-Fifth
Congress of the CPSU

WITHDRAWN

WITHDRAWN

The
TWENTY-FIFTH
CONGRESS
OF THE CPSU:

Assessment and Context

Alexander Dallin, Editor

Hoover Institution Press 1977
Stanford University • Stanford California

781262

The Hoover Institution on War, Revolution and Peace, founded at Stanford University in 1919 by the late President Herbert Hoover, is an interdisciplinary research center for advanced study on domestic and international affairs in the twentieth century. The views expressed in its publications are entirely those of the authors and do not necessarily reflect the views of the staff, officers, or Board of Overseers of the Hoover Institution.

Hoover Institution Publication 184

© 1977 by the Board of Trustees of the
Leland Stanford Junior University
All rights reserved
International Standard Book Number: 0-8179-6842-3
Library of Congress Catalog Card Number: 77-2445
Printed in the United States of America

Contents

Tables	vii
Preface	ix
Contributors	xi

1 Soviet Party Congresses: Intended and Unintended Consequences — 1
William Zimmerman

2 The Twenty-Fifth Congress: Domestic Issues — 7
George W. Breslauer

3 The Brezhnev Regime and Directed Social Change: Depoliticization as Political Strategy — 26
Gail Warshofsky Lapidus

4 Science Policy and Soviet Development Strategy — 39
Paul Cocks

5 The Soviet Economy Before and After the Twenty-Fifth Congress — 53
Gregory Grossman

6 The Military in Soviet Politics: From the Perspective of the Twenty-Fifth Party Congress — 79
Roman Kolkowicz

7 Foreign Policy: The Soviet Union and the Noncommunist World — 89
Paul Marantz

8 Foreign Policy: Communist States and Parties — 95
Jan F. Triska

9 Implications for Soviet-American Relations: Informal Comments — 100
Helmut Sonnenfeldt

Appendix: The Central Committee of the CPSU	109
Notes	111
Abbreviations and Glossary	123
Index	125

Tables

Text Tables

1 The Politburo of the CPSU Central Committee (1976) 36
2 The Secretariat of the CPSU Central Committee 37
3 The Soviet Economy, 1960–1980: Performance and Plans 60
4 1976 and 1980 Target vs. 1971–1974 and 1976 Results 63
5 The Year 1980: A Revised Prognosis 66
6 Annual Agricultural Production and Procurements
  (1971–1980) 72

Appendix Tables

  I Occupations of CPSU Central Committee Members 109
 II Size of CPSU Central Committee 109
III Continuity of CPSU Status 109
 IV Full Members of CPSU Central Committee, by Affiliation
    or Role 110

THE TOP COMMUNIST PARTY LEADERSHIP, 1976

Left to right: M. V. Zimianin, K. F. Katushev, I. V. Kapitonov, K. U. Chernenko, K. T. Masurov, M. P. Georgadze, A. A. Gromyko, Iu. V. Andropov, D. F. Ustinov, V. I. Dolgikh, B. N. Ponomarev, N. V. Podgorny, M. S. Solomentsev, L. I. Brezhnev, M. A. Suslov, P. N. Demichev, V. V. Grishin, A. Ia Pel'she. *(Photo by V. Yegorov, TASS from Sovfoto)*

Preface

The Communist Party of the Soviet Union held its Twenty-Fifth Congress in Moscow from February 24 to March 5, 1976. The Party congress is convened every five years and is the highest formal body to which the Soviet leadership is accountable; in the past, the Report of the Central Committee, delivered by the Party's General Secretary to the congress, and other speeches have often provided important policy statements and clues to changes—or continuity—in domestic and foreign policies. The congress also deals with economic matters; their centrality has been underscored since the timing of five-year plans has been made to coincide with the schedule of Party congresses. The congress elects a new Central Committee, which in turn formally designates the Politburo and Secretariat. It also acts as host for and hears from foreign delegations.

It thus seemed appropriate to make the Twenty-Fifth Congress the occasion for a one-day conference to review its record, assess its significance, and place it into a broader framework of trends in Soviet politics, economy, and society. We are grateful to the Center for Russian and East European Studies at Stanford University for providing the support which made possible the holding of such a conference on April 2, 1976. Enough interest was aroused by the conference to suggest that the participants' remarks should be made more widely available in the form of a book.

The contributors have, of course, been free to revise and extend their comments as they saw fit. Some have elaborated on them at length, while others did not choose to do so. Our authors have pursued their topics in their own and different ways, and this is as it should be. Some papers are more technical than others; others are more impressionistic or comprehensive. They all deserve to be read with care. In fact, the attentive reader may discover differences in interpretation among them.

While the scope of the papers varies, it is interesting that most of the authors found it appropriate to go beyond the congress itself to understand its significance. This approach was particularly suitable because the Twenty-Fifth Congress was relatively lacking in novelty or fireworks. It thus provided an occasion, for us, to try to place the orientations and policies of the Brezhnev regime in a historical and political context.

No effort has been made here to provide a factual summary of the congress' day-by-day proceedings. These can be found, in Russian, in the daily press—such as *Pravda* and *Izvestiia*—for the dates of the sessions. The major speeches and resolutions were subsequently published in book form as *Materialy XXV S"ezda KPSS* (Moscow, 1976). In English, the proceedings are available in the daily issues and special supplements of the FBIS (Federal Broadcast Information Service) *Daily Report: Soviet Union* (U.S. Department of Commerce, National Technical Information Service). Key documents and condensed versions of speeches appear in English in *The Current Digest of the Soviet Press,* a weekly sponsored by the American Association for the Advancement of Slavic Studies (XXVIII:8–17 [March 24–May 26, 1976]). The principal speeches and documents also appeared in English as Special Issues 1–3 (1976) of the *Information Bulletin* of the *World Marxist Review* (North American edition, Toronto, Canada).

Special thanks are extended to the chairmen of the conference sessions, Professors Terence L. Emmons and Wayne S. Vucinich, of Stanford University; and to Mrs. Betty Herring, who handled the variety of technical, logistic, and clerical problems with customary dispatch. Above all, the editor's gratitude goes to the authors, who did not know what they were getting themselves involved in; they came through with flying colors.

ALEXANDER DALLIN

January 1977
Stanford, California

Contributors

GEORGE W. BRESLAUER is Assistant Professor of Political Science at the University of California, Berkeley. In 1975–1976 he was a National Fellow at the Hoover Institution. He has been working on "Transformation and Adaptation in the Soviet Union Since Stalin."

PAUL COCKS is a Research Fellow at the Hoover Institution and Lecturer in Political Science at Stanford University. He has published studies on the Soviet Communist Party, on civil-military relations, and science policy in the USSR.

ALEXANDER DALLIN is Professor of History and Political Science at Stanford University and Senior Research Fellow at the Hoover Institution. He is the author and editor of a number of studies in Soviet politics and history and in international relations.

GREGORY GROSSMAN is Professor of Economics at the University of California, Berkeley. A specialist in comparative economics, he is a leading expert on the Soviet economy and the author of a number of studies of it.

ROMAN KOLKOWICZ is Professor of Political Science at the University of California, Los Angeles. The author of a major study of Party-military relations in the Soviet Union, he has also published widely on Soviet military and arms control policy.

GAIL WARSHOFSKY LAPIDUS is Assistant Professor of Political Science and Sociology at the University of California, Berkeley. In 1974–1975 she was a National Fellow at the Hoover Institution. She is the author of a forthcoming volume on Soviet women and of papers on Soviet politics, education, and social change.

PAUL MARANTZ is Assistant Professor of Political Science at the University of British Columbia. In 1975–1976 he was a National Fellow at the Hoover Institution. He is the author of a forthcoming book on Soviet doctrine and East-West relations.

HELMUT SONNENFELDT is the former Counselor of the Department of State. He has taught at Johns Hopkins University and served the U.S. Government in the Arms Control and Disarmament Agency, the National Security Council, and the Department of the Treasury. Currently he is with the School for Advanced International Studies, Johns Hopkins University.

JAN F. TRISKA is Professor of Political Science at Stanford University. He has published widely on communist affairs, Eastern Europe, and Soviet foreign policy and has had a special interest in the international communist movement.

WILLIAM ZIMMERMAN is Professor of Political Science at the University of Michigan and Director of its Center for Russian and East European Studies. He is the author of a seminal study of Soviet perspectives on international relations and of other papers on Soviet and American policy.

The Twenty-Fifth Congress of the CPSU

chapter one / *William Zimmerman*

Soviet Party Congresses: Intended and Unintended Consequences

The story of the historical evolution of Communist Party congresses in prerevolutionary and Soviet Russia has been told many times.[1] Rather than deal with it to any extent here, suffice it to say that there was a time when congresses really did decide major issues; that is, they performed major policy-making functions. Many of the defining episodes in the history of the Bolsheviks revolved around a Party congress: the Second Congress dispute between Lenin and Martov (1903), and the Tenth Congress clash between Lenin and the Workers' Opposition (1921) are among the best known. Even in more recent times, long after congresses lost their policy-making function, they have in practice either been or symbolized major events in the evolution of the Communist Party of the Soviet Union (CPSU) and the Soviet Union itself; the best known illustration is the Twentieth Party Congress (1956) with Khrushchev's "secret speech," the attack on the cult of Stalin, and the revision of the inevitability-of-war doctrine. Other congresses have also been an important part of the chronology.

We can safely assert that the Twenty-Fifth Congress of the CPSU has *not* been one of such historical magnitude to place it along with such truly great events as the Second, Tenth, or Twentieth Congress or even the Twenty-First (1959) and Twenty-Second (1961). Consequently, the main point here is to explain why, given the evolution of the congresses' functions over time, we should be interested in a congress and especially in this particular congress.

The answer lies in considering both the *intended* functions that we and the Soviet leadership ascribe conventionally to Party congresses and those functions of the Soviet political system, now served by a Party congress, that are largely *unintended* by the Soviet leadership. The latter, I believe, are of greater interest than the former for the study of Soviet politics, especially as the transformational dimensions of the Soviet system gradually atrophy.

Conventional Functions

One conventional function performed by a Party congress is that of elite-mass communication and, in a somewhat different respect, elite-elite communication. Party congresses have traditionally set the "general line"; what is intriguing about the general line in regard to foreign policy as it emerges from Brezhnev's speech at the Twenty-Fifth CPSU Congress is that it is so vaguely and instrumentally formulated that almost any likely policy move over the next five years could be justified by reference to the Twenty-Fifth Congress. The masses have been told that there will be more of the same, but not what "more" (or even "the same") entails.

Party congresses convey a sense of what kind of party will rule the Soviet Union and by what criteria the elite wish to have Party performance measured. This point becomes clearer if we ask, "Why do they bother to have a congress?" The answer, I believe, is that this leadership wishes to convey a sense of predictability. It assumes that it governs better if it transmits the impression that the time is past when a man (or a few men) would act without any restraint, and that certain procedural norms are being observed. This congress, moreover, has been linked with the new economic five-year plan (FYP)—which will henceforth be the continuing practice. I take it that this is intended to reinforce the increasingly routinized and nontransformational style and purpose of governance and to link Party performance explicitly to development and production.

A second function usually ascribed to a Party congress is that of reaffirmation and relegitimation. A congress provides a marvelous opportunity to reinforce, through massive publicity, the authority of the Party and its successes. Indeed, the very composition of the congress reflects a selection of the powerful and "emulatable" in Soviet society—thus providing widely publicized role models for the bulk of the Party's membership.

A third function which congresses provide is to serve as a context for mobilization—an opportunity (even at the pettiest level) to insist that regime commitment be demonstrated by sprucing up the dormitories, cleaning the streets, and performing all sorts of functionally equivalent acts of affirmation in institutes, shops, farms, and ministries; in short, to insist that Soviet reality, however briefly, mesh with its romanticized portrayal.

A fourth traditional purpose—one served by this congress as well—is that they provide the institutionally legitimate context for carrying out personnel changes. A new Central Committee of the CPSU is elected. Professor Jerry Hough has suggested how important that is with regard to an incipient succession.[2] What needs to be added is that the congress is merely the forum which rubber-stamps decisions made in the Politburo and Secretariat. Similarly, the congress provides an occasion for shifts in the composition of the Politburo such as the removal of Dmitrii Poliansky.

A fifth, quite different, but conventionally noted function of the Party congress is its role as a rally of the faithful. I would not dismiss this purpose too lightly. For a sizable fraction of those who attend the congress, it is a "big deal"—in effect, a payoff for achievement or for service.

Finally, there is at least one other major function which congresses are traditionally said to perform. From this perspective, the Twenty-Fifth will be remembered because that function was *not* served. Conspicuous by its almost complete absence was a discussion, much less expostulation, on doctrinal issues.[3] Brezhnev's report to the congress illustrates this point nicely. It reads like a combination of one of Premier Aleksei Kosygin's usual speeches and an American party platform: there will be 37 per cent more horse manure in the new five-year plan and 67 per cent more paper work. . . . There are messages to some thirty foreign states by name—one imagines a member of Brezhnev's staff saying, "I think we ought to include a sentence for the Canadians this year, don't you, Il'ich?" There are routinized statements about women, labor, and scientists. One almost expects to read "Blacks, Chicanos, and Puerto Ricans."

Like the putative Soviet audience, I found myself reading Brezhnev's report with baited breath—though I was holding mine eagerly waiting to see whether he would mention Lenin by name. Had I been at the congress, I would have turned blue long before it happened. Although he used the adjective *Leninist* (much as we used *Bicentennial*), Brezhnev did not mention Lenin by name in the entire first half of a long speech; he finally did so well into the second part. Where Brezhnev speaks in doctrinal terms at all, it is (1) in vague references to the Western economic situation, as illustrative of the general crisis of capitalism, but in a manner not wildly divergent from the way many of us might characterize the events of the past several years, and (2) in reference to notions like proletarian internationalism and continued adherence to it, which he defends on the power-pragmatic ground that it has served its purpose: "From our viewpoint, the renunciation of proletarian internationalism would mean depriving the Communist Parties and the workers' movement in general of a powerful and tested weapon." The nearest thing to theoretical profundity which he articulates is to remind the comrades that there is nothing so practical as good theory—thus putting the General Secretary in the mainstream of modern, pragmatic social science. . . .

Unintended Functions

The congress may also be seen to have served other purposes as well, and these are more interesting.

First, it is an arena for intra-Soviet dialogue about many of the key issues of contemporary Soviet politics—for instance, the Brezhnev cult and economic priorities. There are nuances to be detected in the speeches and comments of Politburo members, republic Party secretaries, and the like, either at the congress itself or immediately thereafter. I doubt if we will remember this congress for something as dramatic as Molotov's minority perspective at the Twentieth Congress or the sharp differences over the treatment to be accorded to the so-called "anti-Party group," which were discerned at the Twenty-First Congress; but a careful reading does give us and the attentive Soviet public a sense of the intra-elite dialogue.

Second, in a more clear-cut way, Soviet congresses—and this one in particular— have become important arenas for dialogue between the leaders of the CPSU and foreign communists. Recent historic examples come immediately to mind: the Chinese and the Albanians quarreling with the CPSU in 1961 and the Cubans speaking out on Vietnam in 1966. Without treading on Jan Triska's prerogative, [4] mention should be made of the Italian and Rumanian delegates' speeches. The Italian speech will no doubt be remembered as the first, however oblique, defense of NATO at a Soviet Party Congress. In some respects, however, the speech by Nicolae Ceausescu, in the name of the Rumanian Communist Party, was even more remarkable.

To convey a sense of how deftly Ceausescu engaged in a delicate balancing act of blending pro-Soviet and distinctly Rumanian (and often anti-Soviet) positions, imagine yourself as a Soviet delegate to the

Twenty-Fifth Congress of the CPSU. In the following statements by Ceausescu, think of which would warrant Soviet applause and which would be greeted with stony silence.

[1] I am particularly pleased to point out that relations of fruitful, comradely cooperation and collaboration in the economic, scientific-technical, cultural and other spheres are developing between Rumania and the Soviet Union in the spirit of the old traditions of friendship and solidarity between our parties and peoples, and that this fully accords with the interests of both countries and with the cause of socialism and peace.

[2] We are expanding cooperation with developing countries and, at the same time, economic exchange with all countries regardless of their social system—including the developed capitalist states—by participating actively in the international division of labor.

[3] Dear comrades: From this platform I would also like to point to the comradely relations existing between the Rumanian Communist Party and the CPSU and to express our determination to continue advocating the uninterrupted development of our parties' friendship, cooperation and solidarity.

[4] The Rumanian Communist Party is developing close relations of friendship, cooperation and solidarity with all communist and workers' parties and acting with the aim of strengthening the cohesion of the international communist and workers' movement, and creating new unity based on respect for the right of every party independently to elaborate its own political line and revolutionary strategy and tactics and creatively to promote the development of Marxism-Leninism and the enrichment of the theory and practice of revolution and socialist construction. We are taking an active part in the preparations for the conference of European communist and workers' parties, wishing to contribute to the fruitful and democratic exchange of experience and opinions among parties and to the strengthening of their solidarity and cooperation.[5]

I believe the juxtaposition of these paragraphs from Ceausescu's speech makes several points.

First, the effect of the statement was predictable. (Needless to say, the first and third paragraphs received the applause.) I coded all the paragraphs in Ceausescu's speech as pro-Soviet, neutral, or anti-Soviet, and then I noted the applause or lack of applause as recorded in *Pravda*. The fit was virtually perfect:

	Applause	*Silence*
Pro-Soviet	9	0
Neutral or ambiguous	1	2
Pro-Rumanian	0	9

More important for the study of Soviet politics is a second point. Soviet congresses have come to acquire a curious function in Soviet society as a consequence, ironically, of the disarray within what used to be called the world communist movement. The Party congress has become one of the few opportunities for Soviet audiences to acquire a sense of non-Soviet but communist approaches to the major issues of the day.

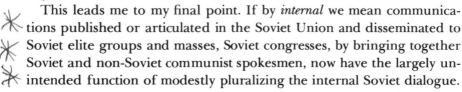

This leads me to my final point. If by *internal* we mean communications published or articulated in the Soviet Union and disseminated to Soviet elite groups and masses, Soviet congresses, by bringing together Soviet and non-Soviet communist spokesmen, now have the largely unintended function of modestly pluralizing the internal Soviet dialogue.

chapter two / *George W. Breslauer*

The Twenty-Fifth Congress:
Domestic Issues

With the coming of the Twenty-Fifth Congress of the CPSU, Leonid Brezhnev, as the General Secretary, has reached the point of having led his Party even longer than did his predecessor, Nikita Khrushchev. And, unlike Khrushchev, it would appear that only voluntary retirement, disability, or death will oust Brezhnev from power in the coming year or two. If anything, his power is being still further consolidated—a conclusion that is reinforced by recent purges in Donetsk *Oblast'* and by the effusive praise of Brezhnev's leadership at the Party congress.

Observers of Soviet politics—journalists and kremlinologists in particular—have traditionally watched for evidence of conflict within the Soviet leadership and have often used it to support conclusions about instability and political change in the USSR. But rather than speculate about immediate political instability, perhaps we should begin by attempting to explain the remarkable stability and continuity that have marked the Brezhnev era.

The clues, I believe, are to be sought in the distinctive ethos of the Brezhnev administration. We have now heard or read Brezhnev's main report delivered to three Party congresses and have listened to him and his colleagues speak on innumerable other occasions. In most cases, one is struck by the uniformity of the ideas, terminology, and approaches— and by the differences between these concepts and those articulated by Nikita Khrushchev. Khrushchev emphasized inordinate optimism about the attainment of social and economic transformation. He intervened continuously in the implementation of policy; he believed in the use of unremitting pressure to attain goals, and he accused Soviet officials of malfeasance when these goals were not attained. When frustrated by the

Special thanks are given to two sources: Professor Alexander Yanov, for comments on an earlier draft of this paper; and the Hoover Institution, for a National Fellowship during the academic year 1975–1976 when this paper was written.

slowdown of the Soviet economy, Khrushchev violated the norms of collective leadership and "mobilized the masses" for attacks on the main institutional bases of power in the system.

In contrast, the Brezhnev administration has continually scaled down its economic targets, in order to bring them more into accord with the capabilities of the Soviet economy. It has abandoned the use of "revolution from above" as the instrumentality of social transformation; and it has reduced the pressure on Soviet executives to attain unprecedented results. In place of Khrushchev's tendency to blame cadres for failures, we have now read for eleven years of the need for "trust in cadres," for a "scientific" approach to decision making that appreciates the "complexity" of problems, that is "realistic" about the capabilities of the system, and that relies upon the fruits of the "scientific and technological revolutions" as the main lever for raising labor productivity. In practice, this has meant the protection of local party and state officials from uncontrolled mass criticism of their political prerogatives, a marked diminution of turnover among high-level party and state officials, and regularization of consultation between Soviet officials and the scientific community. Then, too, we see evidence that norms of collective leadership at the top are indeed being respected and that Brezhnev refrains from excessive interference in operational decision making.

The pattern of rule, then, remains elitist, with the officials who constitute the elite being given security against attacks from above (i.e., personalistic rule) and below (i.e., mass mobilization). Perhaps the ethos of the regime is best summarized in the rather technocratic phrase that has dominated Soviet ideological literature since 1965, "the scientific management of society."

This phrase combines the notions of scientific expertise and hierarchical authority. The Leninist emphasis on manipulation of the masses remains a central tenet, for the notion of "management of society" implies a search for effective methods of societal guidance from above. The notion of "scientific management" combines the traditional Marxist emphasis on rationality and optimism with the current recognition of the need for greater inputs of professional competence to improve the relevance and effectiveness of policies adopted. In political terms, therefore, the Brezhnev-Kosygin years represent a coalition of officials and professionals, with neither group dedicated to the democratization of the system. Rather, they seek to regularize the processes of consultation between officials and experts, in order to improve the administrative effectiveness of Soviet public administration, and to provide a stream of material benefits to themselves and "the masses."

How broad and how stable is such a coalition of political forces likely to be? It would appear that current priorities and perspectives have a very broad appeal indeed. Most of the Soviet population, I would guess, is more interested in material and physical security than in political democratization—and this is precisely what the Brezhnev administration has offered them. Similarly, Soviet officials must be grateful for the more stable and predictable task environments in which they are allowed to work—and for the advantages of material reward, power, and official status that they enjoy. Finally, most Soviet professionals appear to be content with greater opportunities for research, diminished dogmatic control over their conclusions, and greater access to decision makers within their realms of specialization. At least for the foreseeable future, this atmosphere is likely to compensate for what they know to be their subordinate political status vis-à-vis Soviet officials who, after all, control the reins of power.

If these assumptions about the preferences of various groups in Soviet society and politics are correct, then there would appear to exist in the USSR a condition that theorists consider necessary for the maintenance of a relatively stable bargaining structure: a basic agreement "about the nature of the political community, the governmental regime, and the bases of current governmental policies."[1] Such an agreement on context, of course, does not mean consensus on policies. Yet it is precisely such an agreement on fundamentals that makes possible those ubiquitous features of politics: bargaining, compromise, logrolling, shifting alliances, and the like. And it has been this agreement on fundamentals, I would argue, that explains the stability of the Brezhnev regime since 1964.

This situation may be changing, however. Whereas the Brezhnev-Kosygin regime guaranteed a stable bargaining structure for more than a decade by formalizing the power of Soviet officialdom, it has been unsuccessful in attempting to redefine authority among groups *within* the elite—and thereby to improve the efficiency of the Soviet economy. The defense of traditional political jurisdictions and institutional prerogatives has had its most telling effect in three realms of policy: administrative reform; investment priorities; and relationships among the nationalities. In this chapter, I will argue that the program of the Twenty-Fifth Party Congress with respect to the first two of these issues reflects a retreat from the program of the Twenty-Fourth Party Congress, and that Brezhnev's speech reflects his impatience, defensiveness, and dissatisfaction with this retreat. Toward the end of the chapter, I will explore changes with respect to nationalities policies and Brezhnev's efforts to prevent a similar retreat from his recent program in this area of policy.

The Twenty-Fourth Party Congress

In his report to the Twenty-Fourth Party Congress,[2] Brezhnev had thrown his political weight behind a reform of the administrative structure that has come to be known as the production association (ob"edineniia) movement. These associations are conglomerates of several merged enterprises, often crossing both ministerial and regional jurisdictions, that bring under one roof disparate but interrelated industrial processes. Through such a process of concentration, associations reap the benefits of economies of scale, specialization, shorter lines of communication, and a general reduction in the costs of administration.

In order to have a substantial impact on the efficiency of the Soviet economy, though, the administrative reform would have to meet at least two conditions. First, associations would have to be set up in ways that placed criteria of economic efficiency over the protection of political bailiwicks: "Soviet economists stress that reorganization must be an optimizing process. Prior administrative (geographical or ministerial) boundaries should not be an obstacle to rational combinations of enterprises."[3] Second, once established, the associations would have to be given considerable latitude and autonomy from outside pressure and dictates, so that association directors might act as they see fit to increase economic efficiency within their domains.

At the Twenty-Fourth Party Congress, Leonid Brezhnev spoke in relatively forceful terms about the need to meet all these conditions:

> The intensified concentration of production is becoming a necessity. Accumulated experience shows that *only* large associations are able to concentrate a sufficient number of skilled specialists, to ensure rapid technical progress and to make better and fuller use of all resources. The course aimed at the creation of associations and combines must be pursued more resolutely—in the long run, *they must become the basic economic-accountability links of social production.* In creating associations it is especially important that administrative boundaries and the departmental subordination of enterprises not serve as obstacles to the introduction of more efficient forms of management. [Italics added.][4]

The message being conveyed was that the merger movement was more than just a redrawing of the organization chart: it had *political* implica- tions in calling for a redefinition of political jurisdictions and a diminution of political intervention in operational decision making.

At the same Party congress, Brezhnev also announced a change in investment priorities, an "alteration in national-economic proportions," which would entail a "shift to a certain preponderance in the growth rates of Group 'B' " industries. What this meant in practice was a five-year plan which, for the first time in Soviet history, called for the output of consumer goods to grow at a faster rate than the output of producer goods. The result of this change, Brezhnev declared, would be an economy capable of "saturating the market with articles of consumption." Moreover, "an increase in the well-being of the working people" was declared to be "the main task of the Ninth Five-Year Plan." And to underscore that this was not mere rhetoric, the General Secretary spelled out the implications of this commitment for heavy industry:

> Heavy industry must substantially expand the production of means of production for the accelerated development of agriculture, light industry, and the food industry and the still greater development of housing construction, trade, and everyday services to the population. This is precisely the ultimate function of heavy industry.[5]

Following this statement, Brezhnev quoted at length from the works of Lenin to supply ideological justification for his position—a technique generally resorted to in Soviet politics when the speaker wishes to throw his full political weight behind a proposal.

It is not difficult to guess at the motivation behind the changes proposed in 1971. In the eyes of the regime, the maintenance of mass quiescence is dependent upon the system's ability to provide material outputs at a level consistent with popular expectations. The maintenance of intra-elite morale and legitimacy hinges in part on a sense of security that the system is in fact providing those outputs. Yet, by 1971, it had become clear to all involved that the economic reforms of 1965 had not improved the efficiency of the Soviet economy and that a very real economic slowdown had in fact set in. Worker riots in Poland in December 1970, moreover, revealed the potential implications of immobilism on the issue of economic or administrative reform.

Despite this recognition of the need for reform, Brezhnev's proposals met a sad fate during 1971–1976. Powerful forces within the Soviet bureaucracy successfully delayed and distorted the creation of production associations. Their establishment is far behind schedule, and in many cases they have been set up in such a way as to avoid violating the political prerogatives of ministries and provincial Party organizations. As for budgetary priorities, both impersonal economic forces (harvest failures, bad weather, labor constraints, and the like) and political forces (such as claims on resources by the military and heavy-industry lobbies) have effectively reversed earlier hopes for preponderant development of consumer goods output. Indeed, the Tenth Five-Year Plan for 1976–1980 recognized this reversal and even projected still lower rates of growth of consumption than had in fact been realized during 1971–1975.[6]

Brezhnev's Partial Retreat of 1976

Since these trends have so obviously undermined the approach forcefully defended by Brezhnev at the previous congress, we are naturally led to ask questions about their impact on Brezhnev's political position. (1) Are these trends likely to have undermined the legitimacy of Brezhnev himself, his coalition in the leadership, or his program generally? (2) How has Brezhnev responded to recent trends? And (3) what does this portend for the maintenance of a stable bargaining structure within the Soviet leadership?

Brezhnev's speech at the Twenty-Fifth Party Congress,[7] I would argue, clearly indicates that the General Secretary has been thrown on the defensive, but it also indicates that he is counterattacking. On the one hand, Brezhnev has accepted (or has been forced to accept) the unraveling of his program of 1971; but, on the other hand, he has adopted a strategy of warning Soviet officials that time is running out and that basic choices about the *political* character of administrative reforms cannot be postponed for long.

On the issue of production associations, Brezhnev's speech was conspicuous for its benign tone. He mentions, for example, that "more and more production and industrial associations are being created," adding later that "we must . . . remove the burden of inconsequential matters from the upper echelons of management, . . . complete work on the creation of production associations and improve their activity." But nowhere do we find the strong, politicized terminology of 1971. Nowhere does he refer to associations as the only way to concentrate production for the sake of efficiency. Nowhere does he claim for them the status of eventually becoming the "basic economic-accountability links of social production." And nowhere does he refer to (or complain about) the protection of traditional political jurisdictions in the establishment of *ob"edineniia*.

A still more forceful retreat is evident in regard to investment priorities. The "main task" of the Tenth Five-Year Plan is no longer to raise the standard of living or the rate of consumption; it is rather to increase "efficiency and quality" through "technical re-equipment and modernization of industry." Raising the standard of living is now explicitly relegated to the status of a "long-term goal," while heavy industry is no longer called upon primarily to serve the consumer goods industries. Quite the contrary:

> The essence of the Party's economic strategy, permeating both the Tenth Five-Year Plan and the long-term plan, is *a further buildup of the country's economic might, the expansion and fundamental renewal of production assets, and the ensuring of stable, balanced growth for heavy industry—the foundation of the economy.*

Brezhnev acquiesced in the notion that reforms would not challenge the established authority relationships or budgetary priorities of the system and launched his counterattack. As at previous Party congresses, he called for clarifying the rights, responsibilities, and jurisdictions of Soviet managers as the primary means of fostering administrative responsibility; but he now upgraded the importance of this demand by dubbing it "the essence of organizational questions" and the "foundation of foundations of the science and practice of administration."

In a similar vein, the General Secretary bemoaned irrationalities in the existing system of success indicators and incentives, and he lent his support to the further development of mathematical economics and automated control systems as a means of improving the quality of central planning, concluding, "It is important *not only* to remember that the final aim of production is to satisfy certain social needs *but also* to draw practical conclusions from this." [Italics added.] He went on to characterize the need for some form of administrative reform as "an unpostponable matter" which must "take effect in the immediate future." Of course, he assured his listeners that he was no harebrained schemer à la Khrushchev: "The Central Committee is against hasty, impulsive reorganizations of the administrative structure, of existing methods of economic administration. It is necessary to measure the cloth not seven times, as the saying goes, but eight or even ten times before cutting."

This much said, however, Brezhnev immediately went on to indicate that there had already been enough experimenting: "But once we have done the measuring, once we have understood that the existing economic mechanism has become too tight for the developing economy, we must fundamentally improve it." To underscore the point, Brezhnev explicitly threatened to replace "trust in cadres" with more drastic measures: "In the party, a solicitous, thoughtful attitude toward cadres has been solidly confirmed. . . . This by no means signifies, however, that under the pretense of consolidating our cadre pool, those who, as they say, do not pull their own weight, do not fulfill their duties, can remain in their leading posts." And lest his words be forgotten in the interval between his main report on February 24 and his short concluding statement on March 1, Brezhnev returned to the theme in his concluding remarks: "We will act correctly, in a Leninist fashion, if, having acknowledged our achievements, we concentrate attention on the remaining shortcomings, on unresolved tasks."[8] This was the first Party congress of the Brezhnev era at which the General Secretary included such a caveat in his concluding statement.

In discussing resource allocation, Brezhnev's reaffirmation of priority for the development of heavy industry also forced him onto the defensive. Long associated with a highly capital-intensive program for the industrialization of agriculture, Brezhnev could expect to come under fire either from those favoring greater attention to light industry or from those opting for decentralization of initiative in agriculture (the "link" system) as a means of cutting agricultural expenditures. In light of recent agricultural failures, it is clear that Brezhnev's program has come under fire from *both* quarters.

The evidence can be found in Brezhnev's speech. The General Secretary reaffirmed his strategy of industrializing agriculture, calling it a "state task of all the people," and adding that the success of the program "will require time, labor, and enormous investments." Lest any comrades question the wisdom of the program, Brezhnev used very strong language to underscore his commitment. The current approach, he asserted, "completely accords with the fundamental interests of the collective farm peasantry and the working class, has passed the test of time, and has received the approval of all the people. This means it is correct. This means the Party will, in the future as well, follow this line."

Of course, efficient use of agricultural investment will require that the Party "improve the organization and administration of agricultural production." But, perhaps in response to those who favor wider introduction of the "link" system (which has been highly successful where experimentally introduced), the General Secretary added that "this is a complex matter; there are no ready recipes."

A less capital-intensive approach to agricultural development would free up scarce resources for other sectors of the economy—light industry, in particular. While we do not know whether those supporting "ready recipes" in agricultural organization are also those inclined toward heavier investment in light industry, it is at least plausible that this would often be the case. And in this respect, it is worth noting that Brezhnev and Kosygin had very different things to say on the question of resource allocation.

Brezhnev admitted that the slow development of light industry (Group "B")[9] is cause for concern. But he dismissed the arguments of those who placed the blame on the agricultural crisis: "It is not just a question that because of the shortage of agricultural raw materials caused by the poor harvest, light industry and the food industry failed to meet planned indices for a number of products. We must raise this question more broadly and more pointedly." More broadly and more pointedly, Brezhnev laid the blame on attitudes rather than on objective conditions, and pointed a finger of accusation at "central planning and economic organs," the ministries, and all those who "plan and direct this sector of the economy." Rather than calling for expanded investments in Group "B" industries, the General Secretary emphasized the existence of "huge reserves" that could be brought to bear to improve the efficiency of this sector.

Premier Kosygin had very different things to say.[10] While supporting a "continuation of the line in favor of real redistribution of accumulated resources to the advantage of agriculture," he did not refer to agriculture as an "all-people's task" and, unlike Brezhnev, he did not refer to heavy industry as the "foundation of the economy." Moreover, he rather obviously contradicted Brezhnev in his explanation of difficulties in Group "B" industries. In Kosygin's speech we find no attempt to blame the ministers charged with directing these industries, but instead we find the Soviet Premier arguing that current *agricultural problems* "could not but reflect on the rates of growth of the food and light industries." And whereas Brezhnev emphasized that it was agriculture that required assistance from all branches of the economy, Kosygin argued that "there is practically not a single branch of the national economy that could not take part in producing *consumer goods."* [Italics added.]

It is impossible to know whether Kosygin was polemicizing with Brezhnev on these issues, or whether he was simply placating a different constituency on behalf of a relatively united Politburo. Whatever the case, it is rather clear that varied interests are drawing different conclusions from the current economic slowdown.

The Brezhnev Cult: Conditional Praise

Brezhnev's impatience for results, coupled with his apparent defensiveness, may well explain the blossoming of a real Brezhnev cult at the Twenty-Fifth Party Congress. If the General Secretary is seeking to break through administrative and political resistance to the realization of his program, or if he is trying to counter threats to the legitimacy of his rule, further consolidation of his power would be a logical step in that direction. Indeed, the effusive praise of Brezhnev personally exceeded anything we have witnessed in the Soviet Union since Stalin's death (a pattern, incidentally, that continued in the period following the congress).

For all the praise of Brezhnev, however, there were remarkable variations among the speakers in their adulation of the Party leader. S. P. Rashidov, First Secretary of the Communist Party of Uzbekistan, is an example of the "pro-Brezhnev" extreme.[11] His praise was extensive and effusive; it lauded Brezhnev's personality as well as his speech, called him the "most influential political figure of our time," and quoted an Eastern saying to the effect that the joy of the people is when the state is led by a wise man who loves the people and his country. That Brezhnev is obviously not in formal charge of the state [*vozglavliaet gosudarstvo*] did not seem to deter Rashidov.

Others were far more restrained. P. M. Masherov, First Secretary of the Belorussian Communist Party, praised Brezhnev and his "leading role," citing him as head of the Politburo, but engaged in no extended praise of his person and did not call him (as others would) a "leading politician and statesman."[12] S. F. Medunov, First Secretary of Krasnodar *kraikom,* was even more circumspect, acknowledging Brezhnev's contributions but offering very little praise of his personal qualities.[13] Similarly, A. P. Aleksandrov, President of the Academy of Sciences, conspicuously avoided all personal adulation of Brezhnev, saving all his praise for Brezhnev's *speech*.[14]

Perhaps most typical was a middle position on the issue—one that lauded Brezhnev and his personal qualities, but also extolled the virtues of collective leadership, of a leader who is sensitive to the opinions of his associates, and of a Party command that is aware of and responsive to local needs. There was, for example, a note of genuine gratitude in the remarks of Ia. P Riabov, First Secretary of Sverdlovsk *obkom*: "We constantly received the necessary assistance from the Central Committee of the CPSU, the Politburo, the secretaries of the Central Committee, and personally from Leonid Il'ich Brezhnev. . . . The activity of the Politburo is for us a good example of precise, smooth, and collegial work, combining principled exactingness with necessary attention, respect and trust for cadres. This creates conditions for creativity, initiative, and successful work locally."[15] His remarks were echoed by many others,[16] and especially by members of the territorial Party apparatus—the principal beneficiaries of the policy of "trusting the cadres."

Yet herein lies one of the dilemmas facing Brezhnev in the era of "collective leadership." The territorial Party apparatus forms a considerable segment of the Central Committee *plenum*, and the General Secretary undertakes grave political risks in trying to challenge their traditional political prerogatives and orientations. By advocating a program of capital-intensive development of agriculture, Brezhnev avoids antagonizing the territorial Party apparatus in rural areas. But by advocating major reform of industrial administration (as in 1971), the Party leader threatens his base of support in the urban territorial Party apparatus. Brezhnev's retreat of 1976 may have avoided such alienation. Leaders of the territorial apparatus praised Brezhnev and his colleagues for their "trust" and "active assistance," and frequently criticized the ministerial apparatus and the State Planning Committee for failing to deliver supplies needed to fulfill plans. The clear implication of their statements was that no redefinition of authority relationships is necessary to improve the efficiency of the economy—only more reliable and voluminous delivery of supplies from Moscow. Yet the pouring of more scarce inputs into an inefficient industrial administrative mechanism is precisely what Brezhnev is trying to avoid!

The case of E. A. Shevardnadze, First Secretary of the Georgian Communist Party, provides an excellent example of the perspectives of

regional Party secretaries with whom Brezhnev must contend. Shevardnadze was named First Secretary in Georgia only in 1972 and was
charged with cleaning up widespread corruption in that republic. A
former official of the KGB, Shevardnadze could be expected to enforce
Moscow's priorities in the independent-minded Georgian republic. If
anything, we would expect his speech at the Congress to be tougher and
more demanding of local executives than speeches of other regional
secretaries.

Yet, in Shevardnadze's speech before the Twenty-Fifth Congress,[17] we
are offered a fascinating example of the dual roles this man feels he
must play. The Georgian First Secretary sees himself playing a liaison
role between Moscow and his republic with regard to administrative
control. He must see to it that republic officials are disciplined, responsible, and honest in fulfilling their obligations under the national plan.
At the same time, he wants to make sure that sufficient resources are
allocated by the central authorities so as to make it possible for honest
local officials to meet their obligations. As Shevardnadze sees it, there is
no need to redefine political jurisdictions at the local level. The core of
the problem of administrative responsibility lies in striking a balance
between central demands and local capabilities.

Accordingly, Shevardnadze notes that the recent experience in Georgia
demonstrates the importance of the personality traits of executives
[*licknost' rukovoditelia*] in attaining economic goals, adding, "The experience of the recent past in our republic shows that any compromise in
the sphere of the superstructure of society brings about a fall in
economic potential." On the other hand, Shevardnadze makes clear that
an overemphasis on personality traits is equally dangerous, as he
relentlessly chides central planning organs for failing to deliver needed
resources—even citing by name those ministerial officials who have been
least responsive to local Georgian demands.

Shevardnadze's theoretical conclusion then summarizes the dual perspectives he must balance: "Precisely in the dialectical unity of freedom
and discipline, concern and demandingness, rights and obligations,
all-state and local interests, has there been found, and is there found, the
highest manifestation of . . . Soviet democratism. . . . When these capabilities [of the executive] are harmoniously combined with the objective
laws of development of socialist society [i.e., rational supply allocation]
. . . the problem of forward movement is solved."

Political Interests

One of the more difficult and hazardous tasks facing the analyst of Soviet elite politics is that of establishing a link between conflict over specific issues, on the one hand, and changes in ideology or personnel, on the other. Yet, if the interpretation of programmatic conflict developed in this paper is correct, it would also explain several other phenomena at this congress. Changes in budgetary priorities, administrative jurisdictions, and political prerogatives have run up against entrenched political interests. If Brezhnev is trying to break through this resistance, he would be advised to sponsor ideological innovations and statements of principle that would dilute somewhat the privileged status and political autonomy of the bureaucratic elite. And, in fact, there is evidence that Brezhnev has adopted such a strategy.

Traditionally, Soviet officials have protected their privileged status and elitist claims by stressing the "class essence" of the state and the continued predominance of the "indestructible alliance of workers and peasants." At the Twenty-Fifth Party Congress, however, Brezhnev commented that the new Soviet Constitution should "record *not only* the general principles of the socialist system, expressing the class essence of the state, *but also* the fundamental features of an advanced socialist society and of its political organization." (Italics added.) In addition, for the first time in Soviet history, the ideological status of the intelligentsia has been upgraded to the point that it is now included in the "indestructible alliance."[18]

Finally, in the realm of personnel changes, it is worth noting that G. V. Romanov, First Secretary of the Leningrad Party Organization, was elevated to the status of Politburo member. Romanov has been somewhat unusual among provincial Party secretaries in being a strong and vocal supporter of the *ob"edineniia* movement, and a critic of those forces seeking to strip it of its originally intended content.[19] Romanov's presence on the Politburo may assist Brezhnev in his efforts to break through elite resistance to his reform proposals—and to hold off the more extreme forces on both sides of the political spectrum.

None of what has been said so far is meant to imply that the cohesion of the Soviet political elite is disintegrating or that political turmoil is on the horizon. Indeed, one of the drawbacks of kremlinological research has traditionally been its failure to differentiate destabilizing from routine political conflict. Kremlinologists simply assumed that observable conflict must imply severe conflict over fundamentals—a "mighty clash of opposing forces";[20] otherwise, the conflict would not have been observable. The approach adopted here is somewhat different. Taking conflict for granted as a universal feature of political life, I have sought to disclose the political "contract" that accounts for the stability of the Brezhnev-Kosygin regime over the past twelve years. Within this context I have also been examining sources of conflict over specific issues that *might* undermine the political contract. Whether or not it will in fact do so, cannot be predicted.

Nationalities and Resources

Another issue over which intra-elite conflict may become more intense is the nationalities question and, specifically, its relationship to problems of resource allocation. In 1973, the Soviet leadership published a plan for economic regionalization of the country, and the seven announced regions cut across republic boundaries in order to group sections of the country according to their economic potential, rather than according to formal political boundaries. Speeches at the time made clear that this represented a fundamentally new approach to investment policy. It was indicated, for example, that the "interests" of each republic would henceforth be clearly subordinated to larger, all-Union interests in making decisions on the location of new projects. The standard formulation about combining republic and all-national interests was replaced by a formula calling for treating the country as a "single economic mechanism."[21] Even more pointedly, Brezhnev spoke of the need for "freedom of economic maneuvering," and he insisted that the national economy "is not the sum total of the economies of the individual republics and provinces."[22] The General Secretary reiterated this new perspective at the Twenty-Fifth Party Congress, thereby confirming the status of the change: "The single economic organism which has formed within the bounds of the whole country is a firm material base for the friendship and cooperation of our people."

These are the words of a regime that is trying to free its hands of political constraints and to allocate resources among the republics as it sees fit. Yet, like most changes in ideological formulae, the operational significance of the new terminology is unclear. If it represents a new posture of redistribution with respect to regional investment patterns, to whose advantage will funds be redirected? And from whom will they be taken?

The clues are to be found, once again, in Brezhnev's speech. Brezhnev has for several years now associated himself with a very costly program for the development of Siberia's natural resources, as well as with a series of expensive schemes for land reclamation and irrigation in the Non-Black-Earth Zone of Russia and in Central Asia. But at the Twenty-Fifth Party Congress, Brezhnev reaffirmed this commitment with special force. The Soviet leader, in terms not present in his report to the preceding congress, promised "new life to vast areas of Siberia, the North, Central Asia, and the Far East." He pointed out that planners are "now going farther and farther to the east and north for petroleum, gas, coal, and ore," and that "a fundamentally new stage in the development of East Siberia's productive forces has been planned." And as for agriculture, Brezhnev proclaimed that "land reclamation in the Non-Black-Earth Zone will get under way on a broad scale. Major new irrigation systems will be constructed in the southern and southeastern sections of the European part of the country and in Central Asia and Kazakhstan."

These are *very* expensive proposals. Siberian development has always been far less cost-effective than investment in the western and north-west regions of the country. Moreover, irrigation projects in Central Asia, given the current water shortage in that area, would require immense expenditures geared toward the diversion of Siberian rivers into Central Asia.[23] Yet in each case these appear to be the proposals with which Brezhnev has identified himself—as indicated by the fact that the First Secretaries of Kazakhstan, Uzbekistan, and Turkmenia all raised the demand for such river diversion in their speeches at the congress, and received "applause" when they did so.[24] Moreover, the "Basic Directions" for the new five-year plan included a demand that the appropriate authorities draw up plans for such river diversion.[25] The funds will have to be found somewhere. . . .

In part, Brezhnev has been trying to couple the issue of détente with his program for Siberian development by involving Western powers in the project—and thereby securing scarce capital and technology from abroad. But this can deal with only part of the need for inputs, and is unrelated to the cost of river diversion, which will have to come from internal sources. Given the current tautness of the Soviet budget, which has been exacerbated by the economic slowdown of recent years, these costs will probably have to be paid through still further redistribution of investments to the disadvantage of the European republics. Perhaps this accounts for the desire for "freedom of economic maneuvering" evidenced since 1972.

We should be careful not to overinterpret the political consequences of such reallocation, however. Inter-republic conflict over scarce resources, after all, is no new thing; Ukrainian leaders have long since been fighting a losing battle to redirect investment away from Siberia or Kazakhstan back toward the Ukraine; elites from the Baltic states and the northwest have attempted to do the same. In like manner, Central Asian leaders have continuously pressed for greater diversification of their local economies and for increased funding of local projects.[26] Nor is such demand articulation done solely behind the scenes; one can find substantial evidence of such overt interest articulation at all Party congresses during the Brezhnev era.[27] Indeed, at the Twenty-Third Congress (1966) the First Secretaries of Uzbekistan and Turkmenia had raised demands for river diversion similar to those put forward in 1976.[28] At that time the issue was postponed, and similar demands were not articulated at the Twenty-Fourth Congress in 1971. But the droughts of recent years, coupled with an accumulating problem of salinity of cultivated lands in Uzbekistan and Turkmenia, have apparently lent greater urgency to the problem.

In light of these facts, it would be irresponsible to conclude that these issues will destroy the consensus which has underlain the bargaining structure since 1964. At the same time, the fact that Brezhnev endorsed an *ideological* change in regional investment policy, and that the high cost of his regional investment priorities comes at a time when the national budget is so severely strained, suggests that political conflict on these issues is likely to intensify—threatening perhaps the viability of Brezhnev's political coalition (and conceivably of his policy of détente).

Whether or not political conflict will intensify to the point of undermining the bargaining structure (contributing, for example, to the emergence of another "charismatic" leader) may well depend upon whether that conflict focuses, not on regional investment vagaries, but on more fundamental issues: the basic economic division of labor within the federation or the official policies of sociopolitical homogenization. Intra-elite conflict over the level of funding for Central Asian cotton-producing projects would seem to be manageable; conflict over whether or not Central Asia should continue in its role as supplier of raw materials to the federation may not be so easy to contain. Similarly, conflict over whether or not to crack down on corruption in the Transcaucasus is one thing; conflict over whether or not to send in large numbers of *Russians* to purge indigenous elites is quite another.

On this score, it is interesting to note that evidence of such fundamental conflict did surface at the Twenty-Fifth Party Congress in terms that, as far as I can tell, were absent at the previous two congresses. First, for the first time in the Brezhnev era, all six of the Moslem and Turkic Party leaders paid tribute to the Russian people.[29] (For example, previously the Tadzhik First Secretary had held out. This change may be meaningless—or it may indicate a heightened sense on the part of Tadzhik elites of the need to demonstrate their reliability.) Second, G. A. Aliev, First Secretary of the Communist Party of Azerbaidzhan, revealed pointedly that he had succeeded in suppressing "anti-cotton sentiments" in his republic, which had "implanted themselves in the recent past." And third, Aliev himself was elevated to the position of candidate member of the Politburo—a position once held by the now-deposed Georgian First Secretary, V. P. Mzhavanadze. That Aliev of Azerbaidzhan, rather than Shevardnadze of Georgia, was given this position may be a reward for his diligence in suppressing challenges to the economic division of labor.

A careful reading of Shevardnadze's speech at the Party congress does indeed suggest that the Georgian may have been passed over precisely because of the way he chooses to define interethnic relations. His speech is also another indicator of possible conflict over fundamentals. As on the issue of administrative reform, the Georgian Party leader demonstrated once again that, although sent in as an enforcer of Moscow's will, he could not do the job unless he also acted as a consensus-builder in the republic. And this, he appeared to argue, required restraint on the part of central Party officials (the vast majority of whom are Russians) in their response to ethnic assertiveness. The evidence for this interpretation can be found in a series of not-so-esoteric statements in Shevardnadze's speech. He extended lengthy praise to the Russians but coupled it with praise of Moscow's nationality policy (and Brezhnev, in particular) for following in the finest tradition of Lenin's letter of 1923 to the Georgian Communist Party organizations. Shevardnadze did not have to explain that this letter informed the Georgians that Lenin was about to prepare a speech defending the Georgians against Stalin's Great-Russian chauvinism. The message could not have been lost on many Party officials.

What the Georgian First Secretary had given with his right hand, he had taken back with his left.

What did Shevardnadze have in mind in making these comments? Obviously, we cannot interpret his motives with any measure of certainty. Nonetheless, it is at least plausible to suggest that the senior Georgian Party official is appealing against Russianizing forces within the central leadership—forces that were probably strengthened by revelations of widespread corruption in Georgia. Since the vast majority of Georgian Party and state officials are Georgian by birth, it would be natural for officials in Moscow to conclude that such corruption is fostered by ethnic and familial ties and that it ought to be combatted through vigorous Russianization of personnel, selective population movements, and/or expanded Russification in language and educational policy. Moreover, these and other officials might use the evidence of corruption as arguments for redistributing investments to the relative disadvantage of the Georgian republic.

Shevardnadze is caught in the middle. He is clearly in favor of stamping out corruption, but he must also build a clientele of trusted associates—officials with whom he can work and who are capable of administering their republic with some honesty and efficiency. Given his liaison role between Moscow and a proud, independent people, a program of Russianization or Russification cannot be in Shevardnadze's interest, as he sees it. It would alienate him from the bases of support he needs to develop in Georgia. Perhaps he is counting on Brezhnev to restrain the Russifiers, while he seeks to demonstrate that he can clean up corruption without exacerbating the nationality question.[30]

And Brezhnev would appear to be obliging. If the dominant political forces in Moscow are attempting to suppress opposition to the current division of labor, and if some of them favor Russification as one means toward this end, then Brezhnev's statements about national relations become somewhat more explicable. As the perennial coalition-builder, attempting to reorient investments without creating serious sociopolitical problems, Brezhnev has once again adopted a dual posture: endorsing the need to treat the country as a "single economic mechanism," but attempting at the same time to hold back the forces of Russification. For, in contrast with his speech at the Twenty-Fourth Congress, Brezhnev did *not* single out the Russian people this time for special praise—even though more republic Party leaders praised the Russian people at this Party congress than at either of the previous two.[31] Brezhnev's position would appear to be that more funds must be pumped into Siberia and Central Asia to make them better able to fulfill their function as suppliers of raw materials for the nation, but that there must be no challenge to the division of labor *as well as* no Great Russian backlash against the increasingly articulate and assertive ethnic elites. Such a backlash, he might add, would create conflicts of such intensity that they could become unmanageable.

Conclusion

"Scientific management," then, has its greatest appeal when confined to the rationalization of means in pursuit of commonly held goals. It assumes that established authority relationships and political jurisdictions can accommodate policy changes sufficient to maintain the legitimacy and effectiveness of the system. It also assumes that protection against arbitrary rule and political democratization are adequate guarantees of a stable bargaining structure within the elite. But its capacity for consensus building is diminished when hard choices about priorities and prerogatives are at stake, and when highly contentious issues (such as the division of labor, Russification, or major economic reform) enter the political arena.

And herein lies the political dilemma facing Leonid Brezhnev. He needs to challenge traditional political prerogatives to effect the economic reforms that he claims are necessary to improve the efficiency of the economy and to assimilate Western technology. At the same time, he wants to prevent other kinds of contentious issues from becoming salient. In light of the interconnections among all these issues, and given the array of political forces in Moscow, it may not be possible to exercise control over the rate at which problems become issues. Leonid Brezhnev has thus far been successful in pushing the less divisive (but nonetheless contentious) components of his program: importation of Western technology; industrialization of agriculture; regional investment in Siberia and Central Asia. He has been moderately successful in preventing highly divisive issues, such as interethnic relations, from coming to the fore. But he has been utterly unsuccessful in improving the efficiency of industrial administration by breaking through established political prerogatives and relationships. Brezhnev's clear warning at the Twenty-Fifth Party Congress of the untenability of such a stalemate may indicate that important Soviet leaders believe the issue cannot be avoided for long.

chapter three / *Gail Warshofsky Lapidus*

The Brezhnev Regime and Directed Social Change: Depoliticization as Political Strategy

One of the ironies in the development of the Soviet regime is that a political ideology committed to replacing "government over men" with the "administration of things" should have given rise to a political system characterized by uniquely bitter struggles over policy and power. That these struggles culminated in the destruction of an entire generation of revolutionary leaders personally accused of crimes of state, and that a similar charge should be turned ultimately against the accuser himself, merely confirm the degree to which a "cult of personality" in its broadest sense has been the hallmark of a political system ostensibly devoted to the scientific management of society.

In this respect, the Brezhnev regime presents a novel departure from recent Soviet precedent. One of the most striking features of the Twenty-Fifth Congress was its peculiarly impersonal, ahistorical aura. Only token reference to 1917 connected the Brezhnev leadership to its revolutionary and Leninist past. The political drama of the Stalin era was shrouded in silence, as was the bold thrust of de-Stalinization launched by Khrushchev from that very same podium just twenty years earlier. Only the repeated evocations of World War II, with their direct appeal to martial and patriotic sentiment, attempted to link present with past. Otherwise, history at the Twenty-Fifth Party Congress appeared to have begun with the Twenty-Fourth Congress.

The avoidance of more distant historical referents and the dissociation of the Brezhnev leadership from political and ideological antecedents are more than merely accidental (to use a familiar Soviet expression). They represent, I would suggest, one of the distinguishing characteristics of the present Soviet regime—its deliberate use of depoliticization as a strategy for the management of economic and social change.[1] The effort to play down, if not remove from public view altogether, the ideological and conflict-provoking aspects of policy-formation and of intra-elite relations contrasts sharply with what was a quintessential feature of Soviet political life until recently. Formerly, we could observe the deliberate utilization and accentuation of conflicts over ideology and power as an instrument of political competition and of popular mobilization. Indeed, in a broad historical perspective, the Twenty-Fifth Party Congress may be seen as the expression of a new stage in the evolution of the Soviet system. In its approach to policy making as systematic social engineering, to leadership as conflict management, and to cadre recruitment as controlled mobility, the Brezhnev regime reveals a distinctive set of orientations which distinguish it sharply from both its Stalinist and Khrushchevian antecedents.

Policy Making as Systematic Social Engineering

The effort of the present leadership to defuse overt conflicts over values and priorities is expressed, first of all, in its treatment of questions of economic and social development as problems of scientific management. Permeating the speeches delivered by Brezhnev, Kosygin, and other leaders of Party and state was a fundamental commitment to long-term, patient, and systematic social engineering and a preoccupation with its institutional, behavioral, and attitudinal prerequisites. Unprecedented in recent Soviet history, it evokes—albeit in a very different environment—a strand of early Bolshevism which was submerged with the triumph of Stalin. One must go back to the economic and social planners of the 1920s, and their Party supporters and advocates, to discover the spiritual ancestry and political precedent for current preoccupations and concerns.[2]

The economic and social planners of the 1920s, like the Brezhnev leadership today, saw the essence of socialism in the "scientific management of society." They were groping toward a conception of the USSR as a social *system*, a complex universe of differentiated but interdependent parts. Their central concern was to devise and structure relationships and incentives which would link the interests of each sector with those of the rest. They stressed the fundamental importance of the natural and social sciences in exploring this largely uncharted terrain, and they expected from a socialist system the integration of efforts and the concentration and coordination of resources which would permit an optimal pattern of development.

Critical of those Party militants who brought a siege mentality to the cause of social transformation—and whose efforts in the immediate postrevolutionary period had ended in disaster—the early Bolshevik planners insisted that there were no easy shortcuts to genuine social change. Socioeconomic and cultural transformation was a long-term process which required a sustained investment of effort, resources, and time across a broad and comprehensive front. Appreciative of the complexity of their task, they advocated caution, experimentation, and pragmatism. Patient experimentation with diverse modes of action was vital, accompanied by a careful evaluation of relative costs and benefits, risks and payoffs. Their strategy would rely on the efficient utilization of available resources and on the careful training and selective targeting of cadres. And it would combine central planning and coordination with horizontal integration and local autonomy in order to facilitate the adaptation of central objectives to diverse local conditions, needs, and capabilities.

Stalinism represented the very antithesis of this approach to social change. Its essence was "storming," not planning. It was a compulsive, radical, and coercive effort to achieve a massive breakthrough in a relatively narrow sector of economic and political life, to be accomplished by unleashing militant cadres and unlimited resources for an assault on politically defined goals. Its short time frame expressed an obsession with tempo, a radical impatience with all but maximalist solutions.

Where the architects of social planning had envisaged transformation as a qualitative, comprehensive, and cumulative progression through modest but feasible goals, Stalinism institutionalized an obsession with quantitative leaps toward exaggerated targets in narrow, compartmentalized sectors. In its preoccupation with payoffs regardless of risks, the Stalinist model had no place for patient experimentation or for the rational calculation of costs and benefits. It elicited compliance by creating insecurity rather than stable expectations, relying upon pressure from above, on direct confrontation, on administratively inspired "storming," and ultimately on the use of coercion and terror. It required the massive mobilization of manpower and resources rather than their selective and optimal utilization. And it evolved and perfected an administrative structure of vertical, parallel, insulated, and competing hierarchies in economic and political life, pursuing essentially autarchic goals with a minimum of horizontal coordination and integration, each imposing uniform and centrally determined policies with little sensitivity to local concerns and needs.

The antithetical orientations of these two strategies of revolutionary transformation expressed fundamentally different assumptions about the nature of the political environment. The first approach tended to be associated with the view that the Revolution of 1917 had achieved a decisive alteration of Soviet economic and political life and had set in motion an irreversible, progressive movement toward the achievement of full socialism. The direction of historical development was promising and clear; it remained to channel these trends along an optimal path. This approach stemmed from a fundamental confidence which was not shared by other groups within the Party, who saw 1917 as merely the precondition for socialist development and who insisted that the fundamental breakthrough was yet to come. The failure of radical assault in the immediate postrevolutionary period had served to confirm their conviction that the potential for erosion or reversal of revolutionary gains was always present, and that continued progress required an unremitting struggle against overwhelming odds. Stalin not only shared this sense of danger but deliberately cultivated it, evoking the specter of internal and external enemies to intensify an atmosphere of crisis which would give legitimacy and urgency to "revolution from above."

While the presumed utility of the Stalinist developmental model for the rapid industrialization of relatively backward societies has been searchingly questioned in recent years, it was undeniably evident that changes in the very structure of the Soviet economy and social order made this approach increasingly dysfunctional. Growing economic and social complexity, the exhaustion of formerly unlimited reserves of manpower and natural resources, the rising scientific and technical sophistication of the new Soviet intelligentsia, and the new demands these trends placed upon the political system, all brought to the fore in new circumstances an earlier preoccupation with the scientific management of society. The death of Stalin himself removed the essential condition for the maintenance of the Stalinist model and created new options for his successors.

Khrushchev was unable to exploit these opportunities fully, for reasons we shall return to shortly. Despite his efforts to undertake a far-reaching alteration of Soviet political institutions, priorities and values, he was, paradoxically, compelled to fall back upon many elements of the Stalinist heritage in pursuit of new goals. It was not until the advent of the Brezhnev regime that these new possibilities could be more fully and consistently exploited.

Even a brief review of the thematic emphases of the Twenty-Fifth

Party Congress speeches makes clear the Party's relatively new preoccupation with the institutional, behavioral, and attitudinal requisites of
systematic economic and social planning. In approaching problems of
economic development, for instance, a concern with raising the efficiency and quality of production now supplements the traditional obsession with quantitative indicators. This necessary shift to a more intensive
pattern of development in turn depends upon enhanced capacity to
assimilate the achievements of science and technology, as a long succession of congress speakers pointed out.[3]

In social policy, the image of a solidary society has given way to a
greater recognition of differentiation and diversity, which requires
careful attention to the harmonizing of social and individual interests.
The enhanced recognition given to the social sciences in the formation
of public policy, as well as the new emphasis on "socialist humanism,"
notwithstanding its genesis in ideological competition with the West,
express the new concern of the leadership to find more sophisticated
and effective ways of motivating and channeling human behavior. As
one speaker put it, "It is necessary that we deepen . . . and improve the
science that we might provisionally call the study of man."[4]

Yet another example of new preoccupations emphasized at the
congress was the stress on more comprehensive and integrated planning
of both economic and social processes. The speakers at the congress
were voicing their support for further departures from the Stalinist
model of development in the calls for coordinating agricultural and
industrial development in order to insure "a single . . . approach to the
development of the whole agroindustrial complex"; in the description of
new approaches to urban development which recognize the interdependence of enterprises, social services, and manpower; and in the
insistence that new institutional arrangements are needed to encourage
the interbranch and territorial coordination of the economic system.

The striking resemblance between these preoccupations and those of
the economic and social planners of the 1920s is readily apparent.
Indeed, Brezhnev's reiteration of the need to join the contributions of
the scientific-technological revolution with the advantages of the socialist
system reads like an updated version of Lenin's well-known characteriza-
tion of socialism as "electrification plus Soviet power." It is in this sense
that the partial abandonment of a Stalinist approach to transformation
has opened the way for—indeed, has made imperative—renewed attention to the possibilities of the systematic social engineering envisaged in

early Bolshevism. To that extent, the more pragmatic, experimental consideration of a variety of new departures is predicated upon (1) a willingness to detach policy making from *a priori* ideological commitments and (2) a confidence that these departures will not interfere with the basic developmental trends which are assumed to be carrying the Soviet system in a progressive direction.

Leadership as Conflict Management

The use of depoliticization as political strategy is also manifest in an approach to the problems of political leadership which further distinguishes the Brezhnev regime from its predecessors. Under Stalin, what was proffered as the Party's dramatic revolutionary struggle against the forces of counterrevolution was personified in the battle against Trotsky and in the identification of each of the leading Old Bolsheviks as an agent of subversion and betrayal. The cult of Stalin as the sole source of wisdom and leadership was the corollary of this effort to delegitimize all political alternatives. While Khrushchev explicitly repudiated crucial features of the Stalinist legacy—most importantly, the cult of personality itself—he was, nevertheless, forced back upon elements of the Stalinist style of leadership in the service of very different goals.

Precisely those elements in Khrushchev's personal motivation and perception of political needs that led him to initiate fundamental changes in Soviet institutional structure, policy orientations, and political leadership, also required a direct confrontation with the Stalinist legacy. Yet in the course of this confrontation, Khrushchev found it necessary to strike a balance between the need to further and utilize de-Stalinization and the need to contain it. As we know, such balancing was made necessary by his quest for legitimacy as well as for flexibility and for support of his initiatives. The need to challenge the cult of personality without calling into question the very bases of the Soviet system made the rewriting of history, with its retroactive assignment of praise and blame, as urgent a task for Khrushchev as it had been for Stalin himself.

It became apparent very early in the evolution of the Khrushchev regime that one of the consequences of his initiatives was a sharp polarization of Soviet political life. This polarization expressed itself in the crystallization of two competing policy orientations defined by their relation to Stalinism. Khrushchev risked his own career and the fate of his regime in initiating bold departures from Stalinist precedent: defending a more flexible foreign policy that joined "peaceful coexistence" with the capitalist world to a positive evaluation of neutralism and acquiescence in the need for "different roads to socialism"; proposing a revision of domestic priorities which would shift greater resources to light industry and consumer goods; pressing for a more egalitarian allocation of status and rewards; and supporting a cautious liberalization of intellectual and cultural life, accompanied by the equally cautious rehabilitation of some of Stalin's victims. In doing so, Khrushchev earned the growing hostility of those who defend a continuation of traditional priorities, while he disappointed the advocates of a more comprehensive democratization of Soviet life.

What followed may have been unavoidable, given the nature of the Soviet political system. The unremitting struggle to contain the pressures for further de-Stalinization within acceptable limits, while building a political coalition committed to basic reforms, sapped the attention and energies of the Khrushchev regime. Moreover, the egalitarian and populist thrust of Khrushchev's organizational initiatives and social policies threatened the institutional interests and personal prerogatives of important segments of the political and administrative elite. Forfeiting the support of these groups—support that was necessary if not indispensable for the implementation of his reforms—Khrushchev was forced to fall back upon a self-defeating cycle of hasty improvizations, personal interventions, crash campaigns, and political recriminations. Unable to create a stable coalition in support of his policies, Khrushchev was forced into a highly politicized series of initiatives which promised quick payoffs but heightened his personal vulnerability to failure. Ironically, the conditions of his defeat directly benefitted his successor.

Indeed, the very circumstances surrounding Brezhnev's accession to leadership were an important condition of his ability to circumvent the potentially divisive and destabilizing issues with which Khrushchev had been forced to contend. The fact that Brezhnev was elevated by a consensus of his peers, in the absence of equally acceptable rivals and in the context of an understanding about the need for collective decision making and stability of cadres,[5] automatically endowed the new leadership with a legitimacy which had eluded Khrushchev and for which he had had to struggle. The speedy resolution of the succession crisis itself thus provided the conditions for a more comprehensive departure from the Stalinist style of leadership. It permitted the emergence of a new, broadscale orientation committed to creating a stable climate of expectations within the elite itself, which would in turn facilitate a more systematic, coordinated, and comprehensive modification of inherited institutions, attitudes, and patterns of behavior. In short, the Brezhnev regime could enjoy the luxury of not being compelled, by proximity or political need, to confront overtly the legacy of Stalinism, and it had the political insight to realize that from its own vantage point such preoccupations were both unnecessary and unproductive. Where previous regimes were driven to rewrite history, the Brezhnev regime could largely ignore it.

Thus the curious ahistorical and impersonal aura of the Twenty-Fifth Party Congress reflects both the determination and the ability of the Brezhnev regime to dissociate itself from the intra-elite struggles over political and ideological issues which dominated the Khrushchev era and to emphasize material achievements as a measure of the regime's devotion to national interests in both domestic and foreign policy. The very decision to schedule Party congresses at five-year intervals to coincide with national economic plans is an expression of the effort to provide new benchmarks for the evaluation of regime performance.

Moreover, the Brezhnev regime has deliberately eschewed the politicization of policy issues so characteristic of the Khrushchev era. It has transcended the habitual polarization of the Soviet political spectrum by developing a complex of policies and a coalition of elites that defy classification in traditional terms. As the Congress speeches further confirmed, this sophistication can be seen in the pursuit of détente with the United States, and tacit acquiescence in the pressure for pluralism in the international communist movement, combined with high levels of military expenditure and investments in heavy industry and with the intensification of ideological controls over cultural and intellectual life. Likewise, major investments in agriculture are joined to lower growth rates (once again) in the consumer sector, despite a continuing emphasis on the welfare needs of the Soviet population. Similarly, policies designed to improve the wages and living standards of the most disadvantaged groups in Soviet society, and to enhance access of their children to educational institutions, have been introduced in ways which avoid direct challenge to the status and prerogatives of established elites.

In sum, precisely because the present leadership's commitment to a pattern of social and economic policies does not create undue tensions among the major institutional bureaucracies and does not threaten the interests of crucial groups, it has been possible for the Brezhnev regime to confront the problems of systematic social planning from a relatively stable political base.

Cadre Recruitment as Controlled Mobility

The pattern of recruitment to Party membership and to elite positions characteristic of the Brezhnev regime has both made possible and reinforced the regime's other major initiatives, those pertaining to policy making and to leadership.

The Twenty-Fifth Party Congress marked a milestone in the growth of the Communist Party. Its size had increased some 50 per cent since the ouster of Khrushchev in 1964; one of every three Party members has joined the Party in the Brezhnev years. The total membership of the CPSU was not only the largest yet, in absolute terms—almost 15½ million—but also embraced a higher proportion of Soviet citizens than ever before in its history. Roughly 9 percent of the adult Soviet population are Party members, that is, almost 16 per cent of adult males and almost 50 percent of young males with higher education! Thus, although the Party represents a fairly small and selective elite, in numerical terms, it is heavily representative of educated strata and of the administrative and technical elites of the Soviet population.

Recruitment policies in recent years have given further impetus to these trends by emphasizing individual merit and leadership capabilities more than socioeconomic background. By contrast with the Khrushchev period, new recruits have been drawn heavily from the specialized intelligentsia as well as from skilled blue-collar categories. Finally, the increased emphasis on selectivity and careful screening of candidates for membership and promotion, combined with a slower rate of growth of Party membership in recent years, has contributed to the aging of the Party membership as a whole and to lower representation of younger age cohorts.

More selective and controlled mobility, and greater stability of cadres are further manifested in the composition of the Central Committee elected at the Twenty-Fifth Party Congress, reflecting as it does the occupancy of key positions in Soviet economic and political life. The turnover in Central Committee membership, which has been declining dramatically in the Brezhnev period, reached an all-time low at this congress: 90 per cent of surviving full members of the 1971 Central Committee were re-elected. The extremely high rate of retention of cadres throughout the system which these figures reflect has resulted in a steady rise in the age of the Central Committee, from roughly fifty at the time of Stalin's death to over sixty in 1976.

Within the Central Committee, limited opportunities for mobility were created by expanding the size of the voting membership from 241 to 287. This permitted the promotion of 46 former candidate members, as well as the admission of 36 newcomers. Yet even this limited effort at renewal created a body which stands in sharp contrast with the last Central Committee elected under Khrushchev in 1961. At that time, under 40 per cent of the 175 voting members were previous incumbents and almost one-half the members were newcomers. By comparison, in the present Central Committee, notwithstanding its larger size, 70 per cent of the members are incumbents and only 12 per cent are new-comers. (Needless to say, turnover rates under Stalin exceeded even those under Khrushchev.)

Moreover, the promotion of newcomers to candidate membership in the Central Committee was actually curtailed by reducing the size of this body from 155 to 139. While in 1961 over three-fourths of candidate members were new additions to the Central Committee, in 1976 the proportion declined to half.

The general reduction of turnover rates within the political elite has doubtlessly been warmly received by the incumbents. Not surprisingly, they heaped praise on the Party's General Secretary for establishing "comradeliness, trust, and a respectful relation to people in the Party." To be sure, curtailing high turnover rates (associated with Khrushchev's leadership) may have the immediate virtues of preserving stability at the apex and of limiting a potentially destabilizing competition over power and patronage within the elite. However, the limits placed on the upward mobility of a younger generation of cadres, which now dominates the local and regional Party apparatus, may also serve to heighten the long-run fragility of the present coalition.

Further indication of the extent to which stability of cadres has been a hallmark of the Brezhnev leadership can be found in the pattern of personnel shifts at the apex of the political system. The composition of the Politburo elected at the Twenty-Fifth Congress also shows a consistent effort to contain the potentially divisive effects of competition and conflict by maintaining the continuity, stability, and homogeneity of values and experiences within the elite in approaching the problems of succession.

As is readily seen in Table 1, the aging character of the Politburo is even more pronounced than that of the Central Committee, with six septuagenarians among its twenty-two full members and candidate members, and with an average age of 66.4. Ten of the twenty-two have held their positions for a full decade—surely, a sign of extraordinary longevity in the Soviet context if one recalls the fates of the lieutenants

TABLE 1

THE POLITBURO OF THE CPSU CENTRAL COMMITTEE (1976)

Name	Age	Date of Election	Position
Full Members			
Brezhnev, L.I.	69	1957	General Secretary, CPSU Central Committee
Andropov, Iu.V.	61	1973	Chairman, USSR Committee for State Security (KGB)
Grechko, A.A.[a]	72	1973	USSR Minister of Defense
Grishin, V.V.	61	1971	First Secretary, Moscow *Gorkom*
Gromyko, A.A.	66	1973	USSR Minister of Foreign Affairs
Kirilenko, A.P.	69	1962	Secretary, CPSU Central Committee
Kosygin, A.N.	72	1948-52, 1960	Chairman, USSR Council of Ministers
Kulakov, F.D.	58	1971	Secretary, CPSU Central Committee (Agriculture)
Kunaev, D.A.	64	1971	First Secretary, Central Committee, CP of Kazakhstan
Mazurov, K.T.	61	1965	First Deputy Chairman, USSR Council of Ministers
Pel'she, A.J.	77	1966	Chairman, Party Control Committee
Podgorny, N.V.	73	1960	Chairman, Presidium, USSR Supreme Soviet
Romanov, G.V.	53	1976	First Secretary, Leningrad *Obkom*
Shcherbitsky, V.V.	58	1971	First Secretary, Central Committee, CP of Ukraine
Suslov, M.A.	73	1952-53, 1955	Secretary, CPSU Central Committee
Ustinov, D.F.	67	1976	Secretary, CPSU Central Committee[b]
Candidate Members			
Aliev, G.A.	53	1976	First Secretary, Central Committee, CP of Azerbaidzhan
Demichev, P.N.	58	1964	USSR Minister of Culture
Masherov, P.M.	58	1966	First Secretary, Central Committee, CP of Belorussia
Ponomarev, B.N.	71	1972	Secretary, CPSU Central Committee (International Dept.)
Rashidov, S.R.	59	1961	First Secretary, Central Committee, CP of Uzbekistan
Solomentsev, M.S.	63	1971	Chairman, RSFSR Council of Ministers

[a]Died, April 26, 1976.
[b]Appointed Minister of Defense upon Marshal Grechko's death, April 30, 1976.

TABLE 2

THE SECRETARIAT OF THE CPSU CENTRAL COMMITTEE

Brezhev, L.I.	
Suslov, M.A.	
Kirilenko, A.P.	Members, Politburo
Kulakov, F.D.	
Ustinov, D.F.	
Ponomarev, B.N.	Candidate Member, Politburo
Kapitonov, I.V.	Party personnel
Dolgikh, V.I.	Heavy industry
Katushev, K.F.	Communist bloc
Zimianin, M.V.	Ideology and media
Chernenko, K.U.	Party organization
Riabov, Ia.P.	Defense industry
	(appointed October 26, 1976)

NOTE: Names appear in rank order of official CPSU listing.

serving both Lenin and Stalin in the decade after their respective deaths.

The Party congress further confirmed another developing trend: despite evidence of political differences over a broad range of domestic and foreign policy issues the Politburo appears to be a relatively stable coalition of major institutional groups offering considerable support to Brezhnev's leadership. Several key personnel shifts carried out at a special *plenum* of the Central Committee in April 1973 appeared to solidify support for Brezhnev, especially through the demotion of those whose views were known to be at variance with Brezhnev's policies (such as Shelest, the head of the Ukrainian Party organization, and Voronov, advocate of a fundamental reform of agricultural organization). The simultaneous promotion of the Chairman of the KGB and of the Ministers of Foreign Affairs and Defense (Andropov, Gromyko, and Grechko) to full Politburo membership, along with the elevation of the head of the Leningrad Party organization (Romanov) to alternate status, further strengthened Brezhnev's position.[6] By coopting into the top leadership the representatives of key institutional bureaucracies assumed to support a tough approach to foreign policy and a tightening of ideological discipline, Brezhnev was in a better position to deflect criticism of his policies and to portray them as enjoying a broad base of support.

The additional changes in Politburo membership announced at the Twenty-Fifth Congress—the promotion of Romanov to full membership and the simultaneous elevation of Ustinov, with his long experience in retail meat prices (now heavily subsidized), considerable importation of meat, rationing, or some combination of these.

In this connection, one should take note of a passing hint in the "Basic Directions" that some retail prices may be officially raised. In recent years, there have been official price increases for a number of significant commodities, in addition to which there has been a constant, unpublicized upward drift of prices in general. Now, the policy is formulated as "ensuring the stability of state retail prices of *basic* food and nonfood commodities" [emphasis added] while reducing prices of some commodities "as supplies permit."[43] The implication here is that state retail prices may be allowed to rise on *nonbasic* commodities—but we have just seen that meat prices may also rise. A greater degree of flexibility of official retail prices would help the planners bring about a more orderly distribution of commodities and more efficient use of resources, especially during times of significant structural readjustment such as now exist. But in this regard, Soviet planners have been severely constrained by the internal political risks of dealing with a public long assured that inflation has no place under socialism.

Overhanging the official retail market and greatly complicating the task of the planners are the very large liquid savings in the hands of the public, mostly held in currency or in deposits at state savings banks. If currency holdings have been increasing at a rate close to that experienced by savings banks deposits, which does not seem implausible, then the total liquid savings of the public have been rising over the past fifteen years at a fairly steady annual rate of 15 per cent. This is to be contrasted with an average annual rate of growth of legal money incomes of $7-7.5$ per cent.[44] The resulting high public liquidity of consumers constitutes a growing threat of disruption to official markets in the event of some shock. The same high liquidity may also be at once a cause and a consequence of the seemingly growing volume of illegal and semilegal activities of all kinds, the so-called "second economy" of the USSR, which often is a boon to the consumer and the harried manager but is doubtless also a legal and political problem of the first magnitude for the authorities.

Little Prospect of Economic Reform

The Tenth Five-Year Plan, while less ambitious than its predecessor, must still contend with a continued deceleration in the rate of growth of resources. As a result, it stresses improvements in labor productivity and

Twenty-Fifth Congress signals that an aging leadership, which has been in power for almost a dozen years and which is beset with a host of recalcitrant domestic problems, has run out of bold initiatives and would be quite satisfied with a policy that sees the slow accumulation of further gains abroad rather than any dramatic breakthroughs.

Massell, *The Surrogate Proletariat: Moslem Women and Revolutionary Strategies in Soviet Central Asia, 1919—1929* (Princeton: Princeton University Press, 1974).

3. [See Chapter 4.]

4. Speech by E. A. Shevardnadze, First Secretary of the Georgian Communist Party (*Pravda*, February 27, 1976).

5. For the view that Brezhnev's accession was accompanied by an "implicit compact" within the leadership which imposed certain conditions upon Brezhnev, see T. H. Rigby, "The Soviet Leadership: Towards a Self-Stabilizing Oligarchy?" *Soviet Studies*, October 1970.

6. Andropov's promotion to full Politburo membership was of further significance in establishing a pattern of KGB representation which was subsequently followed at the republic level in a number of cases.

Chapter Four (Paul Cocks)

1. "Science policy" is used here as a shorthand term for science *and* technology policy. Given the strong accent on technical modernization and applied R & D for economic, social, and political purposes, the term in the current Soviet context refers particularly to technology.

2. *XXV s"ezd KPSS: Stenograficheskii otchet* (Moscow: Politizdat, 1976), I, 82.

3. See his report to the Twenty-Eighth Belorussian Party Congress, *Sovetskaia Belorussiia*, February 5, 1976.

4. See *XXII s"ezd KPSS: Stenograficheskii otchet* (Moscow: Politizdat, 1962), I, 238—39.

5. See Andrei Sakharov, Roy Medvedev, and V. F. Turchin, "Letter of Appeal of Soviet Scientists to Party and Government Leaders of the USSR," March 19, 1970, reprinted in *Survey*, no. 76 (Summer 1970), pp. 161—70.

6. L. I. Brezhnev, *Ob osnovnykh voprosakh ekonomicheskoi politiki KPSS na sovremennom etape: Rechi i doklady* (Moscow: Politizdat, 1975), I, 418.

7. *Pravda*, June 13, 1970.

8. See particularly the excerpts from his speeches at the December 1973 and 1974 Central Committee meetings, published in his *Ob osnovnykh voprosakh*, II, 341—61, 443—49.

9. *XXV s"ezd KPSS*, I, 64.

10. Ibid., p. 72.

11. Ibid., II, 239.

12. Some light was shed on this point shortly after the congress by the Chairman of the State Committee for Science and Technology that oversees these programs. Briefly, the number of key problems has been reduced to around two hundred. Each program, as a rule, concludes with a specific result. Deadlines are set for intermediate work stages as well as for final completion, and all necessary financial, material, and technical resources are provided.

the defense industry—clearly represented a continuation of the
established trends as well as an effort to broaden the experience of two
promising leaders, possibly as a step in preparation for even higher
positions in the future.

In sum, the Congress might have offered an unprecedented occasion
for measures to facilitate an orderly transition of power in the years
ahead, both through an institutionalization of mechanisms for the
succession and through the promotion of a younger cohort of Party and
state officials to Politburo and Central Committee membership. But the
leadership chose instead to minimize the risks of destabilization, which
such initiatives might invite, by giving greater emphasis to the retention
of experienced cadres in order to maximize continuity and homogeneity
in the short run. In doing so, it may have risked a greater future
vulnerability by creating insufficient opportunities for the upward
mobility of a younger generation of cadres and sharpening the cleavage
between central and local elites.

The pattern of cadre recruitment and promotion which has
characterized the Brezhnev regime is both consistent with and
supportive of the basic tendencies in policy making and in leadership
which we have been exploring. In fact, it may be said that these three
basic departures marking the Brezhnev 'regime's political style—its
approach to policy making as sytematic social engineering, to leadership
as conflict management, and to cadre recruitment as controlled
mobility—have been mutually reinforcing and, therefore, have helped
to endow the Soviet system with a relatively greater stability and
flexibility than it has heretofore possessed.

chapter four / *Paul Cocks*

Science Policy and Soviet Development Strategy

In the sphere of science policy[1] the significance of the Twenty-Fifth Congress is best understood if the congress is seen not as an isolated event but rather as part of a broader unfolding strategy of modernization, designed to overcome the technological backwardness and bureaucratic inefficiences of the Soviet system. More and more, the key to this strategy—the "decisive element" (to use Brezhnev's expression) which links technology and development—is organization.[2] As P. M. Masherov, First Secretary of the Belorussian Party and candidate member of the Politburo, observed shortly before the congress, "The deepest roots of our success, of our failures and of our capabilities are to be found precisely in the organizational factor."[3] There were no radical new departures, no "great leaps forward" at the congress. At the same time, it would be misleading to see only inertia and inaction, only the great gaps but not some steady gains. Though cautious and conservative, the measures adopted by the congress represent the reaffirmation of a political commitment to the acceleration of scientific and technical progress, as well as small, incremental but determined steps to achieve it. Underlying this commitment is the hope that modern technology and organization can help solve the basic economic, social, and political troubles of Soviet society.

The Twenty-Fifth Congress in Perspective

The great attention given at the congress to issues concerning science and technology in domestic and foreign policy reflects the extent to which a perceived "technological imperative" has come to dominate and divide the Kremlin leadership in the last decade. As long as fifteen years ago, modernizing pressures were beginning to build within the ruling elite. These pressures surfaced during the debate in 1961 on the new

draft Party Program, Khrushchev's blueprint for "building communism" by 1980. Significantly, at the top of the list of amendments,
which the Central Committee accepted and the Twenty-Second
Congress then approved, was the proposal to lay stronger emphasis on
the importance of accelerating technical progress and making fuller and
more rational use of productive capacity. A special clause was also added
to the program on the conservation of nature and the proper utilization
of natural resources.[4] There was an emerging awareness, at least in some
official circles, of the two big issues of modern industrial society,
technology and ecology. However, in 1961 they were only dimly
perceived, much less understood. The Party Program projected
essentially a continuation of the high rates of growth and basic patterns
of production, which were characteristic of the 1950s, at a time,
ironically, when the Soviet economy was already approaching the limits
of "extensive" growth and entering a new era that called for more
"intensive" methods of development.

The needs of modern society that were only faintly glimpsed by a few
in the Soviet Union in the early sixties, however, have become more and
more apparent to the ruling group as a whole in the seventies. They find
partial expression in the "basic directions" for the Tenth Five-Year Plan
(1976–1980), which were approved by the Twenty-Fifth Party
Congress. The official labeling of this plan as "a plan of efficiency and
quality" reflects clearly the perceived tugs of technology. Similarly, for
the first time, a special section has been introduced into the five-year
plan on environmental protection and improving the use of natural
resources.

Adjustments in perceptions and policies have not been rapid or easy,
however. Politicians have lagged rather than led in the awakening to the
full significance and sweep of the so-called "contemporary scientific and
technical revolution" (hereafter abbreviated as STR). Not surprisingly, it
was among the Soviet scientific community that concern mounted over
Russia's backwardness and the growing technological gap with the West.
Thus a letter of appeal from dissident but concerned scientists to Party
and goverment leaders in March 1970 noted frankly, with respect to the
computer age: "We are simply living in a different era. The second
industrial revolution came along and now, at the onset of the seventies,
we see that far from having overtaken America, we are dropping further
and further behind."[5] Generally speaking, the notion of the STR, which
has become the buzzword of the Brezhnev regime in the 1970s, had

been primarily a subject for academic debate in the 1960s. At the Twenty-Third Party Congress (1966) Brezhnev did not mention the term. Kosygin, who seems to have been more aware then of the changing conditions and new demands of the times, used it twice but very generally and only in passing. Not until the 1971 congress did the scientific-technical revolution begin to emerge as a fundamental organizing concept for Soviet domestic development and foreign relations. It is Brezhnev who emerges more and more as the principal champion of the pursuit of technical progress with the general outlines of a broad modernization program.

The basic ideas underlying this strategy began to take shape and find expression in Brezhnev's speeches the year prior to the Twenty-Fourth Congress. A major turning point, it seems, was the December 1969 Central Committee *plenum*, where he declared firmly that intensification "becomes not only the main way but the only way of developing our economy and solving such fundamental sociopolitical tasks as building the material-technical base of communism, raising living standards, and achieving victory in the economic competition between the two world systems."[6]

Six months later he stressed, "The solution of many economic problems should now be sought at the junctures between scientific-technical progress and progress in management." He also made the statement which has since become a slogan of the times, namely, that "the science of victory [in building communism] is in essence the science of management."[7] Two key factors of "intensification," two main sources of future economic growth, are increasingly singled out and stressed by the General Secretary: modern technology and modern management. The linchpins of his grand (or should one say grandiose?) strategy become the "management of science" and the "science of management." Moreover, after the Twenty-Fourth Congress he continued to stress not only their importance but also the impossibility of having one without the other.[8]

These are basically the major ideas that punctuate and dominate Brezhnev's report to the Twenty-Fifth Congress. Just as he had defined the acceleration of scientific-technical progress to be the "key task" of economic policy five years before, so he now listed it first among the "key problems" of economic development. Similarly, he repeated the point he had made five years earlier, that the main thing now was not individual scientific achievements, no matter how brilliant, but a high scientific-technical level of production. Again he stressed—and the congress reaffirmed—the historic importance of "organically combining the achievements of the STR with the advantages of the socialist economic system," adding the qualifier that this task be done "consistently." To make it perfectly clear to all the delegates that he regarded the success of science and the success of socialism as inseparable, the General Secretary reiterated the position he had expressed the previous October at the two hundred and fiftieth anniversary celebration of the USSR Academy of Sciences: "The building of a communist society can be attained only on the basis of the accelerated development of science and technology."

One senses in Brezhnev's remarks that perhaps his greatest disappointment (if not defeat) was the absence of a comprehensive fifteen-year economic development plan for the USSR as the main item of business on the agenda for the Twenty-Fifth Congress. This had been one of his pet projects ever since its endorsement by the last congress. He regarded it, apparently, as a "second Party program" and perhaps as his own blueprint for building, if not communism, then at least an advanced stage of developed socialism. Since 1972, work on such a development plan that would extend to 1990 has been underway. Given the tremendous and recurring difficulties the leaders have in trying to devise feasible five-year plans, however, it is no wonder that such long-range planning has encountered stiff resistance. To many members of the Kremlin "establishment," the whole venture must appear as an even more harebrained scheme than anything Khrushchev had attempted.

A Three-Dimensional Approach to Scientific-Technical Progress

Broadly speaking, everyone in the USSR is for science, technology, and modernization. There is also general agreement that the process of accelerating and directing scientific-technical progress needs to be improved. This need was echoed by virtually all who took the speaker's podium at the Twenty-Fifth Congress. At the same time, it was also evident that there is considerable dispute over what should be improved and how. Following Brezhnev's lead, the gathering tended to elaborate and extend what may be called a three-dimensional approach to speeding technological advance. Actually, the broad outlines of this approach had been drawn at the Twenty-Fourth Congress and developed further by Brezhnev in the interval between Party congresses. Suffice it to say that this approach emphasizes improvement essentially along three main directions: (1) planning and management, (2) organization and structure, and (3) economic levers and material-moral incentives. To a certain extent, this approach may be viewed as a kind of Kremlin analog of the planning–programming–budgeting systems (PPBS) approach that presidents Kennedy and Johnson championed in the 1960s as the way to use modern technology and management to land a man on the moon or build a Great Society on earth.

More specifically, in regard to planning and management at this congress, Brezhnev continued to press his campaign to extend the horizons of planning beyond the prevailing short-term, incremental mold in order to accommodate the kind of decision making and long lead times inherent in the development of science and technology. He acknowledged that the guidelines for a fifteen-year plan "cannot and should not be as binding or as detailed as those for a five-year plan." But such long-range planing, he stressed, has a different purpose, namely, "to determine well in advance the nature and scope of the tasks facing us, to concentrate efforts on accomplishing them, to see possible problems and difficulties more clearly, and to facilitate the formulation and implementation of programs and projects going beyond the framework of a five-year period."[9] The need for more scientific forecasting and technological assessment to provide a better basis for planning was also endorsed. Brezhnev noted that the Academy of Sciences had, in fact, prepared a draft, "Comprehensive Program of Scientific-Technical Progress and Its Social and Economic Consequences for 1976–1990." He also left a strong impression that he regards this program as "an organic and integral part" of the planning process and the keystone of the fifteen-year economic development plan. As he told the delegates, "It provides points of reference and orientation without knowledge of which it is impossible to manage the economy successfully."[10] The congress, however, indicating that this effort did not yet meet with full approval, instructed the Academy "to continue" its work on this project and "to see to it" that such forecasts "are better grounded."[11]

In addition, the congress gave considerable attention to the need to apply more broadly a "programmed-goals approach" to planning and management. A kind of "programmitis" filled the air as many participants fastened on this management-integrative tool with high hopes of solving more effectively the growing problems of complexity and change. Its use was particularly urged for major construction projects, like the territorial-production complexes being built in Siberia, Central Asia, and the Far East, as well as for large-scale research and development (R & D) programs. Calling for comprehensive programs centering on key scientific, technological, economic, and social problems, Premier Kosygin singled out as priority tasks the development of the nuclear power industry and the mechanization of manual and heavy physical labor. A. P. Aleksandrov, President of the Academy of Sciences, suggested that the intensification of agriculture and development of computer technology be raised to this special national program status. Brezhnev, on the other hand, stressed the particular importance of elaborating comprehensive programs for the development of the fuel and power complex, metallurgy, and the leading branches of machine building.

In regard to science policy specifically, Kosygin told the congress that the new five-year plan will include "for the first time" concrete and integrated programs for solving key scientific and technical problems. Actually both the Eighth (1966–1970) and Ninth (1971–1975) Five-Year Plans had roughly two hundred and fifty such key projects, which consumed about 40 per cent of the total science budget. The extent to which these new "integrated programs" will go beyond the old practice of "coordination plans" and faulty systems management for these priority projects, remains to be seen.[12] Much more than before, the accent is on the actual introduction of scientific results into the economy, on integrating science, technology, and production. The problems of implementation nonetheless remain.

Broader use of the "programmed-goals" approach was not to be limited to "nonacademic science," that is, to the system of applied R & D concentrated in the branch ministries and supervised by the State Committee for Science and Technology. It also extends to "academic" science and the system of fundamental research as well. This point was emphasized most explicitly at a special meeting of the Academy of Sciences that was called at the end of May 1976 to hear a report on "The Decisions of the Twenty-Fifth CPSU Congress and the Tasks of the USSR Academy of Sciences." The congress had added an important clause to the draft guidelines for the economy, noting the need to raise the role of the Academy of Sciences as the center for theoretical research and coordinator of all scientific work in the country. In practice this means, the scientists were told, that the Academy's coordinating functions "should be not the mere recording of innumerable topics but the elaboration of major research programs which are important to the country and the organization of their implementation."[13]

Underlying this heavy stress on the systems approach was the need to deal more effectively with major interbranch problems that cut across ministerial lines. Brezhnev particularly complained about too many "nursemaids," about the fragmentation of decision making and administration, leading to unwarranted cost overruns and protected delays. "What is required here," he told the congress, "are integrated and centralized programs embracing all stages of work, from project design to practical implementation."[14] Others also dwelled on the difficulties of achieving interbranch cooperation and coordination. Not surprisingly, the strongest support for more of a systems approach came from the republic and regional party secretaries in attendance. They also usually coupled their endorsement with criticism of the central ministries for failure and mismanagement of projects located on the territory of their Party committee.[15]

Another important dimension of the "programmed-goals approach" that Brezhnev stressed was the need to focus planning and management more on "end results." "This approach becomes especially urgent," he explained, "as the economy grows and becomes more complex, when these end results come to depend more and more on a multitude of intermediate units, on an intricate system of intrabranch and interbranch ties." "In these conditions," he insisted, "it is easy to overlook the most important thing—the end results."[16]

Taken together, the statements of the General Secretary and decisions of the congress indicate the efforts being made to bring space-age management perspective and technique to the Kremlin. The emphasis on setting objectives, developing action plans, determining the means to accomplish them, and appraising performance on the basis of results is, in essence, the heart of modern management. The "programmed-goals approach" is basically Soviet-style "management by objectives," "results management," and "systems planning, programming and budgeting," to use equivalent Western terms. Much like leaders of complex organizations the world over today, in government and business, Brezhnev and company are attempting to use these tools to improve managerial performance and effectiveness as well as to ensure party control.

In the area of improving structure and organization, the same accent on a broader systems approach dominated the congress proceedings. On the one hand, attention focused on the process of integrating science with production through the creation of industrial, production, and science-production associations. The greater capabilities of these large conglomerates and specialized complexes for systems management and speeding technological modernization were recounted and extolled. The benefits of various organizational experiments and new methods were also described and recommended by numerous speakers. While both Brezhnev and Kosygin lamented the slow pace of restructuring, they noted that steady progress was being made. At the beginning of 1976, the number of production associations and science-production associations had climbed to 2,300. They now accounted for 24 per cent of all industrial output (compared with 10 per cent in 1971 and 14.5 per cent in 1974). In 1975 alone, 600 associations were formed. The process of creating these new basic building blocks of Soviet industry will be completed during the Tenth Five-Year-Plan.

On the other hand, the very delicate issue of restructuring and regulating more effectively interbranch ties also received prominent mention but no resolution. Following up his proposal to establish integrated and centralized programs for major interbranch problems, Brezhnev drew the appropriate organizational conclusion: "It is important that in each case there be specific agencies and specific people bearing the full measure of responsibility and coordinating all the efforts within the framework of each program."[17] During the discussion of Brezhnev's report, Politburo member M. S. Solomentsev strongly endorsed the General Secretary's organizational proposition. "There is nothing of greater urgency," he said.[18] Also sitting as Premier of the Russian Republic, where many of the largest interbranch construction projects and R & D programs are concentrated, Solomentsev knows well the problems of coordination about which Brezhnev ranted. The First Secretary of the Belorussian Party, P. M. Masherov, also came out for major reform. This class of complex interbranch problems, he said, "goes beyond the framework of the possibilities of the USSR *Gosplan* and *Gossnab*." He suggested searching for a better solution, possibly creating, for example, appropriate structural subdivisions within the USSR Council of Ministers that could effectively manage diverse interbranch processes.[19] On this, however, the congress took no action other than to note in the Basic Directions for the new plan the need to improve the structure and functions of the machinery of ministries and of interbranch and functional agencies.

Only brief mention can be made here of efforts regarding the last direction of improvement under this approach to modernization, economic management and incentives. In line with the general thrust of the congress, strong emphasis was placed on tying financing and budgeting—especially in construction—more closely to "end results." In his report, Brezhnev insisted that investments must be allocated to ministries and departments not in lump sums, not for new facilities, but for planned increments in output. Material and financial resources should be channeled first of all into the technical retooling and reconstruction of existing enterprises where production capacities can be expanded without new construction or with smaller per unit capital outlays. Stress was also laid on expanding the use of bank credits for technical re-equipment of enterprises. Economic incentive funds and workers' bonuses are also to be linked more directly to the fulfillment of planned deliveries and of contract terms. (The so-called Zlobin method of team contract used at places in the construction industry and widely advertised at the congress, uses basically a results-oriented appraisal and reward system; this is also largely true of the L'vov comprehensive system for improving product quality and control, which had been approved by the CPSU Central Committee in July 1975 and was strongly promoted at the congress.) To be sure, the congress also heard and endorsed, as usual, calls for enhanced "moral incentives" and "socialist competition" to overcome passivity toward improving output quality, reducing costs, and accelerating technological change. Shortly after the congress, an all-Union "socialist competition" was launched with the aim of fulfillment of targets relating to the most important scientific and technical interbranch problems.[20] Significantly, this class of priority projects in the past was not generally subject to such a form of social and political pressure tactics. It remains to be seen whether this new initiative will help or hinder the execution of science policy.

The Party and the STR

What is the relationship between the CPSU and the STR? How has the Party adjusted to the changing conditions and new demands posed by the STR? Indeed, what is the role and future of the Party in the era of the STR? Significantly, these questions were not addressed at the Twenty-Fifth Congress. In fact, it is the only congress that did not make any changes in the Party rules (bylaws). For that matter, it is the only congress that ever failed to adopt even a resolution on intraparty questions and limited itself to a brief note approving the report of the Central Committee. Except for another, equally short, statement accepting Premier Kosygin's report, the only documents produced by the assembly were the final guidelines for the new five-year plan.

Does the failure of the congress to raise these questions mean that they are simply not important or problematic issues? Does the paucity of discussion about internal Party affairs mean that there is no ongoing debate or political controversy over organizational policy and activities? Does all this mean that the Party is standing still or standing to the side and being bypassed by the scientific-technical revolution?

To this observer, the answer to all these questions must be an unequivocal "no." Issues surrounding the STR and its implications for the future of the Party and the Soviet political system are constantly at the core of Kremlin politics today. There is considerable debate and disagreement within the ruling elite over how to modernize and how to master the STR. In March 1972 and again in July 1973, for example, Brezhnev mentioned that the Central Committee intended to examine soon, at one of its plenary meetings, the problems of accelerating scientific-technical progress.[21] However, no such meeting has taken place. At the same time, the ruling group has faithfully adhered to the policy it laid down soon after Khrushchev's ouster of not publicizing its internal deliberations and policy conflicts. Thus the proceedings of Central Committee meetings are no longer available. In this sense, the Twenty-Fifth Congress, in its relative lack of open display of political controversy and detailed discussion, is very much in keeping with prevailing political practice.

On the other hand, the very neglect of intraparty matters and preoccupation at the congress with science policy and development strategy reflect the extent to which the latter issues have come to dominate the attention and agendas of Party meetings at all levels. At various republic Party conferences that shortly preceded the CPSU congress, numerous examples were cited documenting the close involvement and intrusion of Party authorities in the struggle for scientific-technical progress. In Azerbaidzhan, for instance, the Bureau of the Central Committee began in 1975 to work up annual lists of the most important construction projects and placed their implementation under systematic and strict Party control.[22] In Turkmenistan, permanent commissions to handle various development projects were established within the republic's Party Central Committee.[23] In the Ukraine, the Kiev City Party organization (*gorkom*) was separated from that of the province and made directly subordinate to the republic's Party Central Committee, in order to strengthen Party leadership over the affairs of the capital.[24] Indeed, the local Party authorities in areas like Kiev, Novosibirsk, Sverdlovsk, and especially Moscow and Leningrad, where the bulk of Soviet R & D is concentrated, have taken considerable initiative in promoting technological modernization.

The creation of production associations has also resulted in new organizational forms for improving the activities and coordinating the work of Party organizations at enterprises and R & D units belonging to the associations and sometimes situated in various administrative districts. These include unified Party committees and councils of Party secretaries. At the Twenty-Fifth Congress, I. G. Kebin, the Estonian Party's First Secretary, urged that a nationwide study be made of the positive experience of these new forms of Party work, so that they can ultimately find expression in the Party rules.[25] With regard to the rising number of organizational experiments in both Party and government, however, there still seems to be strong reluctance and resistance to generalizing innovation and change. In a sense, the whole process of experimentation needs to be subjected to a systems approach and be better administered and integrated.

Significantly, Brezhnev himself indicated at this congress that the process of adapting the Party, its political practices and organizational principles, to the new conditions and demands has not been without problems. He singled out two major interrelated areas: (1) Party control and (2) criticism and self-criticism of cadres. With regard to the first, he noted that the CPSU Secretariat had given "much more attention than ever before to control, verification, and follow-up on the implementation of adopted decisions." This subject was also "repeatedly" dealt with at Politburo meetings. Even a special letter, he revealed, had been circulated by the Politburo to all Party organizations on this issue.[26]

Similarly, there had been "serious and principled discussions"— that is, fights and conflicts—at meetings of the Central Committee about criticism and self-criticism with respect to carrying out decisions and responsibilities. "We did this," the General Secretary explained, "because in view of the growing scale and complexity of the tasks with which we have to cope, a critical approach to all matters acquires special importance." But he indicated firmly that there could be little ground for debate, compromise, and foot-dragging here: "It is obvious that, once adopted, decisions must be fulfilled." To be sure, "high exactingness" had to be combined with "trust and respect" for cadres. The thrust of his remarks, however, left little doubt on which side of this equation he stood. Interestingly, Brezhnev concluded his more prefatory remarks to the Central Committee Report with the statement: "I say all this just now not because some sort of alarming situation has developed in our Party regarding the implementation of adopted decisions or the state of criticism and self-criticism."[27]

Obviously, to some Party members, including assembled delegates, it seemed such an "alarming situation" had arisen. From his remarks, we can glimpse that Brezhnev's whole orientation of "management by objectives" and "appraisal by results" is beginning to have an impact upon the political system, upon Party management as well as governmental administration. For a long time, cadre policy and the system of *nomenklatura* regulating appointments and promotions have relied substantially on a system of appraisal by personality traits such as judgment, initiative, alertness, dependability, and loyalty. Now the "programmed-goals approach" and management by objectives call for a shift from personality to performance, where the standards for evaluation become objectives, programs, schedules, cost, and quality. More effective management control systems are needed to enhance responsibility and improve communications, coordination, supervision, and motivation of managers and officials at all levels. Brezhnev's remarks reveal a growing awareness and apprehension that today's problems cannot be readily remedied by available management techniques and methods of Party control. Hence, though "the Party and the STR" was not an official item of business at the Twenty-Fifth Congress, we can be sure that it was a nonagenda issue very much on the minds of many of those assembled in the Kremlin's Palace of Congresses.

Brezhnev's Modernizing Strategy and Tactics of Implementation

Our discussion has tried to draw Brezhnev as a political strategist of modernization. He is a man with a vision and the broad outlines of an action plan, a three-dimensional approach to accelerating scientific-technical progress. He has tried to bring a more modern managerial perspective to the ruling establishment in order to help move it beyond the prevailing system of institutional pluralism, incrementalism, and bureaucratic "muddling through." He has urged a more global, systems view in order to overcome the penchant for "thinking small." Through greater use of long-term planning and forecasting, he has encouraged planners to "think forward" rather than "from the achieved level." With the aid of modern decision-making methods, automated management information systems, and computer technology, he has attempted to promote a more professional and scientific approach to decision making in place of a "seat-of-the-pants" approach. These are his hallmarks as a strategist and political leader who is determined to have the Party master the STR and thus remain the dominant force in Soviet society.

However, Brezhnev also stands out, perhaps even more, as a shrewd political tactician and manager of change. To be sure, at the Twenty-Fifth Congress, he clearly revealed his own sense of disappointment and exasperation over the slow pace of reform. He also gave the delegates the strong impression that he is convinced his development strategy is the right one and it only needs to be implemented. He quoted Lenin's point that, once a correct policy and a sure course have been worked out, success depends chiefly on organization. The General Secretary then asserted, "We have such a policy and such a course. Consequently, the decisive link becomes organization."[28]

Brezhnev's strength as a tactician and innovator, however, lies precisely in his keen understanding of the organizational politics of change. He is very much aware that behind the structural constraints, the so-called "departmental barriers," blocking the implementation of reform, stand invisible mechanisms and political constraints, the so-called "psychological barriers," which must be overcome. It is in his method of coping with the organizational—social—political obstacles to change that Brezhnev, moreover, differs substantially from Khrushchev as a political tactician and reformer.

Broadly speaking, there are three methods of implementing change.[29] The agent of change may rely on the use of raw power and direct orders, persuasion, or education, or a combination of all three. Khrushchev was a reformer who wound up resorting to the tactics of force as his frustration with the Soviet bureaucratic establishment mounted. He pushed for immediate structural change and constant reorganizations in order to improve administrative performance and effectiveness. In the end,

while he often made things different, he did not always make them
better.

Brezhnev, on the other hand, has chosen not to do major battle with
the bureaucracy. He has not engaged in the same kind of high intensity
tactics as his predecessor. He understands better the political character
of the implementation process and is fully aware, it seems, that the
strength of any countermovement is directly related to the intensity of
the attack on the status quo. Consequently, he has adopted a different
set of tactics, namely, the combination of vigorous advocacy, persuasion,
and education. On one level, he has relied on the use of organizational
experiments to help reduce fears of risk and feelings of uncertainty
about change, to help convince conservative critics of the correctness
and benefits of innovation. On another level, he has continued to
promote modern management training and development programs for
both Party and government executives, so they can master the achievements of science, technology, and organization. Since the Twenty-
Fourth Congress, Brezhnev pointed out, more than 230,000 func-
tionaries had taken refresher courses and 40,000 persons had been
trained in the Party's academic institutions alone. Allocations from the
central Party budget for training and retraining of its *apparatchiki* had
grown by 24 per cent in the same period.[30]

In sum, therefore, the Twenty-Fifth Congress generally reflects not
only Brezhnev's modernizing strategy but his implementation tactics as
well. However, one cannot help but note a fundamental inconsistency
between the two. While his strategy emphasizes the need for a total
systems outlook and approach to the problems of Soviet Russia's
development, Brezhnev's tactics recognize the need for a piecemeal,
experimental, and incremental form of implementation—that is, political "muddling through." Certainly, this has been the key to the success of
his survival. Whether or not it will ultimately result in the success of his
strategy remains to be seen. Brezhnev is well aware of what happened to
Khrushchev and his program for "building communism" when he
forced the pace of change. To save himself and his own program, the
General Secretary seems to have taken as his motto Lenin's last words of
advice, "Better Less But Better."

chapter five / *Gregory Grossman*

The Soviet Economy Before and After the Twenty-Fifth Congress

As 1975 slipped into history, the USSR completed its Ninth Five-Year Plan period and started its Tenth. Forty-five years is middle age for an individual; it may also be for the Soviet planned economy—a possibility that appears to be confirmed by the Tenth Five-Year Plan or at least by the outline for it approved by the Twenty-Fifth Congress of the CPSU.[1] Now that the USSR rivals the United States in industrial output, it has used up some of its chief reserves for rapid industrialization; its institutions have become more rigid; both the society and the economy have become increasingly intractable; popular expectations and other pressures are mounting; and the whole economic organism is slowing down markedly.

Many of these trends are not new at all. Some have been in evidence since Stalin's death almost a quarter of a century ago; others are even older. But in one very important respect, the Soviet economy turned a crucial corner in its history only around 1970 when it began to run out of plentiful reserves of labor for industrialization and modernization. Throughout the 1960s, large additions to the industrial labor force were a key ingredient of the Soviet Union's "extensive" formula for industrialization (a formula which also included plowing back a very high proportion of the national product into capital formation, large-scale manpower training, and massive importation of Western technology). By 1970, for both demographic and economic reasons, this resource was greatly depleted. Between 1950 and 1970, total civilian nonagricultural employment had increased at an average annual rate of 3.9 per cent and industrial employment at 3.7 per cent, whereas during 1971–1975 the corresponding annual average rates of increase were only 2.5 and 1.5 per cent, respectively.[2] The prospect for the second half of the 1970s is

An earlier version of this paper appeared in *Problems of Communism*, XXV:2 (March–April 1976). It is reprinted here with the kind permission of the journal's editor, revised and updated as of the end of 1976.

equally tight or even more so in this regard; the Tenth Five-Year Plan implies an average increase in industrial employment of less than 1 per cent per year.[3] And tighter still is the outlook for the 1980s, when the total working population of the USSR will presumably grow between 0.5 and 1 per cent per year, and industrial employment may well not grow at all.[4]

If rather high rates of economic growth are to be maintained—and this is necessary if the economy is to satisfy rising consumer expectations and pressing claims from other economic sectors and interest groups— then the leveling off of nonagricultural employment will have to be offset by a considerable stepping up of the rate of growth of the capital stock (other things, such as average efficiency of resource use, remaining approximately the same). This rate of growth would require even larger and more rapidly growing volumes of annual investment—and even faster rates of technical progress. Yet such a prescription is not an easy one for the Soviet economy to follow. First, the system has not shown itself to be easily amenable to efficient substitution of capital for labor and to rapid technical innovation. And, second, maintaining—let alone accelerating—the rate of capital formation is likely to be difficult in any case.

The proportion of Soviet GNP going into gross investment is already very high and even under favorable circumstances could not be stepped up without impinging on such high-priority sectors as consumption and defense. But conditions are not favorable: the very slowdown of economic growth itself will make this transfer of resources to capital formation even more difficult, both technically and politically. Furthermore, new claims on real investment resources have lately emerged from several quarters. The recent emphasis on motorization calls for large investments in the infrastructure and ancillary facilities of automotive transport, which until recently were mostly ignored. The need to replace depleted traditional sources of energy and other mineral resources has occasioned highly capital-intensive investment, often in remote and frontier areas where wages are high and infrastructure requirements are great; such projects are now doubly necessary to meet the growing needs of the rest of Eastern Europe as well. Rising attention to the preservation of the environment places still other new claims on capital in the USSR as it does in all other industrial countries. Then there is the costly new railroad, the Baikal-Amur Mainline, being built in the wilderness of

Eastern Siberia, and port facilities are being expanded. And finally, there is also agriculture.

The crop failures of 1963, 1965, 1967, and 1972, and most seriously that of 1975 have progressively enhanced the priority accorded to agriculture in the allocation of resources and investment funds. One can now speak of a veritable Soviet "Project Independence," a concerted program designed to achieve fairly dependable and steadily rising grain harvests with a view to future self-sufficiency at high per capita levels of consumption of animal products. It is not a cheap program. Whereas in the second half of the 1960s the share of total gross fixed capital investment going to agriculture averaged 23 per cent, in 1974 it reached 27 per cent.[5] In fact, during the first half of the 1970s, the value of fixed capital in agriculture (exclusive of livestock) grew nearly half again as fast as in industry, though output grew much more slowly in the former sector than in the latter (even if one discounts the effects of adverse weather).[6] For 1976, if one also includes investment going to branches of the economy supportive of agriculture (the tractor and agricultural machinery industries, the fertilizer industry, housing, research institutes, etc.), agriculture was to receive over 34 per cent of the gross fixed investment in the whole economy for the current year. This is a major dent in the country's resources of investment capital, in fact amounting to over 10 per cent of the expected national income (Soviet series) for 1976.[7]

By 1970, moreover, it was already clear that the efficiency of utilization of the USSR's scarce resources was not going to be appreciably improved by the economic reforms launched with some fanfare five years earlier. The most important consequence of the reform had been and would continue to be to heighten the emphasis placed on material incentives as a means of eliciting compliance from the work force at all levels of skill and responsibility and in all walks of life.

The Ninth Five-Year Plan: Ambitious Goals

It was in this setting that the Ninth Five-Year Plan (1971–1975)—the second five-year plan under the Brezhnev-Kosygin leadership—was launched and ran its course. It was an ambitious plan, not so much because the targets were uncommonly high but because the growth of the resource base, especially of the labor force, had already begun to level off. In fact, in percentage terms, most production and real-income targets of the Ninth plan were set very close to the claimed achievements of its predecessor, the Eighth plan (1966–1970)—at times a little lower, but at times even a little higher.[8] During 1966–1970 the total nonagricultural labor force had increased by 19 per cent and the industrial labor force by 15 per cent, whereas for 1971–1975 the Ninth Five-Year Plan envisaged increases of only 13 and 6.5 per cent, respectively. Accordingly, the Ninth plan assumed an acceleration in the rate of growth of labor productivity and large economies in the utilization of major industrial materials and energy. Since the economic reform was already in retreat, such striking qualitative improvements seemed dubious and, therefore, the Ninth plan was widely adjudged by Western observers (and hinted by some Soviet authors) to be ambitious. In any event, it was substantially underfulfilled in various respects, not only in agriculture, of course, where the plan fell far short of its targets.

It is not clear to what extent the drafters of the Ninth Five-Year Plan counted on Western economic assistance in the form of credits, technology, and capital-goods imports. Even the book-length version of the plan, which went to press in April 1972,[9] was still very laconic on economic relations with the West, hinting that these would expand only at a moderate pace. Quite possibly, this stance was tactically motivated: to avoid giving the impression that the success of the plan depended on the West's cooperation. Be that as it may, there is little doubt that, if the Ninth plan stood any chance of coming close to its goals, it needed (in addition to favorable weather) large-scale economic assistance from the West. Conceivably, a very bold and far-reaching economic reform could have boosted the economy's overall efficiency and, in this fashion, could have been substituted for Western help; but such a move has been out of the question in Brezhnev's USSR for internal political reasons. To put it in terms of our opening metaphor, only a massive infusion of technology and resources from the West—if that—could preserve the Soviet economy's youthful élan and rapid growth once it had entered its middle age around 1970. And for this to happen, the West, and especially the United States, had to be persuaded that the international political climate had changed sufficiently to justify large-scale economic assistance to the Soviet Union. Thus the Soviet post-1970 policy of détente, with its heavy emphasis on "normalization" of economic relations, has been quite consistent with the USSR's domestic economic imperatives of the 1970s and 1980s.

Efforts to fulfill the ambitious goals of the Ninth Five-Year Plan met with both bad and good luck. The worst luck came in the form of natural conditions, on top of the usual inefficiencies of Soviet agriculture, that occasioned two severe crop failures in 1972 and 1975. Although adverse weather, especially droughts, have been a recurring phenomenon in Russian and Soviet history, two major crop failures in five years *is* bad luck.[10]

The magnitude of the 1975 catastrophe must be fully grasped. The official Soviet grain crop figure of 140 million metric tons[11] is to be compared with an average crop of 192 million tons over the preceding four years—an average which includes the low harvest of 1972 (168 million tons), at which time 30 million tons were hurriedly purchased in the West. The 1975 figure is also to be compared with the revised target of 215.7 million tons contained in the 1975 annual plan,[12] which would indicate a shortfall of some 76 million tons, or some 60–65 million tons if one allows for normal rates of harvesting waste. (The drought also affected other field crops and pasture, of course, though generally less severely; cotton, on the other hand, did very well in 1975; for details, see Table 6 on page 72.

To gauge the significance of a 60–65 million ton shortfall in grain production, one need only recall that the original target for 1975 procurement of grain by the government from all domestic producers was 87 million tons. Carryover stocks were probably not large owing to the mixed production record of the preceding several years. Thus the 1975 crop failure triggered large new grain purchases in the West, primarily in the United States. However, imports probably cannot come close to filling the gap caused by the latest crop failure, for the shortfall is more than double the reputed annual throughput capacity of Soviet ports; that is, it is more than double what it was physically possible to import during the 1976 crop year. Consequently, a considerable volume of demand did presumably remain unsatisfied until at least the next harvest, resulting primarily in a substantial shortage of fodder for animals, even if possibly not of grain and potatoes for direct human consumption. And indeed, excessive slaughter of hogs and sheep took place in the second half of 1975, which helps explain the high reported production and sales of meat at the time. Production of meat fell sharply in 1976. The consequences of the 1975 grain crop failure were heavily felt in 1976 and will be for some time to come—despite the seemingly good crop that followed in 1976. The 1975 crop failure may have been the largest single blow suffered by the Soviet economy since the German invasion of 1941.

But not all was bad luck. One should note on the positive side the ability and willingness of the West, particularly the United States, to come to the USSR's rescue with grain in both 1972 and 1975. (Moreover, in 1972 American grain was sold to the Soviet Union at bargain prices.) These acts of accommodation on the part of the superpower-adversary—acts for which apparently no political compensations were sought or obtained—surely are worthy of note in the annals of history and in any case must be counted as instances of Soviet good luck.

Another bit of good fortune in the first half of the 1970s was the large amount of credit extended to the USSR by Western governments and private interests for the purchase of capital equipment, often at preferential interest rates and on preferential terms.[13] Lastly, there was the shift in relative prices in world markets after 1972–1973, which—at least initially—heavily favored Soviet exports (including gold). The last two developments should be counted as positive, even though most of the Western capital goods whose purchase was financed by the credits and hard-currency windfall could not have arrived and been put to use in time to affect in any appreciable way the fulfillment of Ninth Five-Year Plan production targets for 1975.

A Plan Underfulfilled

The net result of all these factors—shrinking resources and ambitious planning, bad luck and good—was a considerable underfulfillment of the targets originally envisaged in the Ninth Five-Year Plan. But the student of the Soviet economy is faced with the problem of separating out that portion of the shortfall which derived from longer term retardatory trends in the Soviet economy (and which, as noted previously, probably were not sufficiently reflected in the Ninth plan) from that portion which was ascribable chiefly to nature's lapses.

Some idea of the dimensions of the shortfall can be seen in Table 3. According to the "Basic Directions," total national income utilized (Soviet series) was 28 per cent higher in 1975 than in 1970 (representing a growth of 5.1 per cent per year on the average) instead of the planned 38.6 per cent (6.7 per cent per year). Agricultural production, in average annual gross value terms, increased in 1971–1975 by 13 per cent instead of 21.7 per cent over 1966–1970. Industrial output in 1975 was 43 per cent higher than in 1970 (a growth of 7.4 per cent per annum) instead of a planned 47 per cent (8.0 per cent per annum),[14] and within this category, the figures for consumer goods rose 37 (6.5) per cent against a planned 48.6 (8.2) per cent. Thus, although the Ninth plan was the first in Soviet history to provide for a faster rate of output growth of consumer goods than of producer goods, the actual relationship was the reverse, as usual.

Rarely in the postwar period have such underfulfillments of global production categories been admitted. There is reason to believe, moreover, that these official data—as has generally been true of official data in the past—overstate growth and, therefore, do not reveal the full extent of the 1975 setback and of underfulfillment of the whole five-year program. The Soviet national income series is almost certainly subject to appreciable inflation, perhaps by at least a percentage point per year.[15]

In addition, there is reason to suspect that the claimed growth of overall industrial output—7.4 per cent per year, representing 97 per cent fulfillment of the targeted production level for 1975—is very likely overstated. While the output of electricity and some basic fuels and industrial materials—coal, oil,[16] steel, cement, mineral fertilizers—hit the respective targets or came within a few per cent of them, output of other products, many of more advanced fabrication, generally fell considerably short of their targets, insofar as can be determined. This was true of commodity groups such as nonferrous metals, basic chemicals, synthetics and plastics, paper and paperboard, dairy products, other foods, textiles, footwear, knitwear, and a number of major consumer durables, and—last but not least—machinery.[17]

Most items of civilian producer machinery and equipment fared not too well, despite the high priorities accorded to them. Data for twenty-one such machinery groups indicate a median degree of plan fulfillment of 89 per cent,[18] although the Soviet claim is to have achieved the planned index for machinery and metalworking as a whole.[19] (Incidentally, the increased importation of machinery and equipment from the West, probably above levels anticipated in the Ninth plan, tended to compensate partly for shortfalls in domestic production of such items. This factor underscores the importance of détente for the Soviet economy.)

The USSR claims to have just met the planned volume of gross fixed investment, in ruble terms. However, it is highly doubtful that the target for the real physical volume of capital formation was even approximately achieved. This much is evident from the as yet partial data on capacity installed in various industries in relation to increments planned in the

TABLE 3

The Soviet Economy, 1960–1980: Performance and Plans

Index	Seventh FYP 1965/actual (1960=100)	Eighth FYP 1970/actual (1965=100)	Ninth FYP 1975/plan (1970=100)	Ninth FYP 1975/actual (1970=100)	Tenth FYP 1980/target (1975=100)
National income utilized[a]	132	141	138.6	128	126
Civilian employment, all	113	110	n.a.	n.a.	n.a.
Workers and employees, all	124	117	112	113[b]	n.a.
Fixed capital stock	157	144	n.a.	144[b]	n.a.
Fixed capital stock ("productive" only)	159	148	n.a.	150	n.a.
Energy consumed (calories)	132	125	n.a.	128[c]	n.a.
Investment, gross fixed[d]	145	143	141.6	142	126
Industry:					
Gross output, all branches	151	150	147	143	136
Gross output, Group "A"[e]	159	151	146.3	145	138
Gross output, Group "B"[e]	136	150	148.6	137	132
Ingot steel produced	139	127	126	122	119
Electricity produced	174	146	144	139	133
Fixed capital stock ("productive" only)	168	152	n.a.	147[b]	140
Workers and employees	121	115	106	107	104
Electricity consumed in industry	169	140	n.a.	134[b]	n.a.
Capital/person employed	139	132	n.a.	137	134
Output/capital	89	99	n.a.	97	97
Labor productivity	125	132	139	134	131

TABLE 3 (Cont.)

THE SOVIET ECONOMY, 1960–1980: PERFORMANCE AND PLANS

Index	Seventh FYP 1965/actual (1960=100)	Eighth FYP 1970/actual (1965=100)	Ninth FYP 1975/plan (1970=100)	Ninth FYP 1975/actual (1970=100)	Tenth FYP 1980/target (1975=100)
Agriculture:					
Gross value of output[d]	112	121	123	113	116
Grain output[d]	107	129	116	108	118-21
Agricultural labor force	99	95	n.a.	n.a.	n.a.
Average money wage or salary	120	126	122.4	120	117
Real income per capita	119	133	130.8	124	121
Retail sales, state and cooperative, in current rubles	133	148	141.8	136	129

SOURCES: For results of the Seventh and Eighth FYPs, see official Soviet statistical yearbooks; for results of the Ninth FYP, see sources cited in note 1 for Grossman/Chapter Five; for the Tenth FYP, see "Basic Directions," in *Pravda*, March 7, 1976, as in part slightly corrected later in the year (*Pravda*, October 26, 28, 30, 1976). Data on total civilian employment and agricultural labor force are from M. Feshbach and S. Rapawy, in U.S. Congress, Joint Economic Committee, *Soviet Economy in a New Perspective* (Washington, D. C.: Government Printing Office, 1976), p. 135.

NOTES: Where *n.a.* is indicated, figures were not available.

Figures in italics are extrapolations or computations by the author.

aSoviet concept.

bExtrapolated from 1971–1974.

cExtrapolated from 1971–1973.

dRatios of investment totals or of average annual output for five-year periods ending in the stated year and in the earlier base year.

eGroup "A" is a catchall Soviet category of producer goods, i.e., all manufacturing, mining, and utilities other than those producing finished consumer goods (the latter being designated Group "B").

Soviet aggregative production and productivity claims (the "actual" figures above) usually contain substantial overstatement; however, they may nonetheless be unable to compare trends for five-year periods, as in this table and later ones in the chapter. Western estimates of the average annual growth of Soviet national income or GNP generally fall about 1 percentage point below the official Soviet claims. Thus the average annual rate of growth of "national income utilized" for 1961–1970 implied in the figures above is 6.4 percent; the independent estimate by Stanley H. Cohn for "national income," 1962–1970, yields 5.4 percent ("The Soviet Path to Economic Growth: A Comparative Analysis," in *The Review of Income and Wealth*, March 1976, p. 51).

five-year plan;[20] for fourteen industries, mostly basic materials and
transport, the median percentage fulfillment in this regard is only 66 per
cent. As in previous periods, housing construction fell short of the
target, this time by about 6 per cent. The attainment of the overall target
for fixed investment (in rubles) seems to have been facilitated by chronic
cost overruns, a problem that has attracted much attention in the Soviet
press lately.

We have already adverted to the crop failure of 1975. Its effects on
industrial production (and on consumption levels) may not show up fully
in the 1975 statistics owing to the drawing down of domestic stocks of
foodstuffs and industrial materials and to imports of grain. However,
the uncommonly modest targets of the 1976 annual plan and the corresponding performance in that year (see Table 4) bear witness to the
profound effects of a disastrous crop on the whole economy, both
directly and through such indirect links as the balance of payments.

Increases in labor productivity did not match the optimistic targets of
the Ninth plan,[21] even on the basis of official statements, let alone after
correction for the likely overstatement of global output magnitudes. It is
also probable that the hoped for economies in the utilization of materials
and fuels were not fully realized, in view of the generally poorer fulfillment of plans for production of highly fabricated goods (requiring
inputs of energy and basic industrial materials), compared to the
fulfillment of output plans for energy and materials themselves. The
failure to attain these goals is probably not unconnected with the fact
that during the Ninth plan period (i.e., 1971–1975) the economic
reform was in steady retreat, as already noted—a retreat that in turn
stemmed partly from the ambitiousness of the plan itself, which tended
to heighten the pressure on resources and, therefore, to prompt recen-
tralization in planning and management. (Such reciprocal action between institutions and performance is not uncommon in Soviet
experience.)

This recentralized control was able to muster a certain success. The
Ninth Five-Year Plan's best record may well lie in the least publicized
sector, namely, the munitions industry (see reference 19). Traditional
heavy industry did quite well in relation to the plan, too, as (for a change)
did the production of mineral fertilizers[22]—no doubt spurred by the
pressing needs of agriculture.

Exactly what happened to consumption levels cannot yet be ascer-
tained. The official statistic is that real income per capita rose over the

TABLE 4

1976 AND 1980 TARGETS VS. 1971–1974 AND 1976 RESULTS

(per cent increase per annum)

	1971-1974	1976		1980
	Actual[a]	Target	Actual	Target[b]
National income utilized[c]	5.5	5.4	5.	4.7
Industrial output, total	7.4	4.3	4.8	6.3
in Group "A"[d]	7.8	4.9	5.5	6.7
in Group "B"[d]	6.6	2.7	3.	5.7
Fixed capital investment, gross	6.6[e]	5.1[e]	4. [f]	4.7i[f]
Freight, ton-kilometers	6.6	5.7	4.5	5.4
Agricultural output	3.1	1.9[g]	0.8[g]	2.7[h]
Grain output	9.7	1.9[g]	4.5[g]	2.1-2.5[h]
Average money wage or salary	3.6	2.7	3.6	3.2
Average collective farmer earnings,				
public sector	5.1	5.0	6.	4.4-4.8
Real income per capita	4.4	3.7	3.7	3.9
Retail sales	6.2	3.6	4.6	5.2
Labor productivity				
in industry	5.9	3.4	3.3	5.5
in construction	5.1	5.5	3.3	5.4
on railroads	4.7	3.0	1.3	3.7
Housing construction	0.6	1.5	-0.1	0-1.0[i]

SOURCES: For the 1971–1974 data, see *SSSR v tsifrak v 1974 g.* (Moscow: Statistika, 1975); for 1976 plan targets, see *Pravda*, December 3, 1975; for 1976 results, see *Pravda*, January 23, 1977; for 1976–1980 targets, see Table 3 and sources listed in note 1 to Chapter 5.

[a]Expressed as average annual increase between 1970 and 1974.

[b]Expressed as average annual increase between 1975 and 1980.

[c]Soviet concept.

[d]See footnote "e" to Table 3.

[e]By state only, i.e., excluding investment by collective farms and households, which is relatively small.

[f]All investment (including that by collective farms and households).

[g]1976 in relation to the average for 1971–1974, i.e., excluding 1975, averaged for 3½ years.

[h]Average for 1976–1980 in relation to the average for 1971–1974, averaged over 5½ years.

[i]Five-year total in relation to preceding five-year total.

five years to an index of 124, as compared with the planned level of 130.8; in other words, consumption per capita in 1975 was supposedly 5 per cent short of plan. Domestic production of consumer goods and services generally fell even more below the respective targets, but it must be remembered that an increasingly significant role in the consumption picture is played by imports, quite apart from the emergency grain imports. The shortfall in housing construction has already been noted. In his address to the Twenty-Fifth Congress, General Secretary Brezhnev placed (shifted?) heavy blame for the shortcomings of recent years on those responsible for planning and managing the consumer goods industries.

Whatever the exact increase in average consumption during the Ninth plan—the first five-year plan in Soviet history to hold forth the target of raising consumption as a paramount objective—there is little doubt that it was substantially less than during the preceding five years. (This might have been the case even without the unusually bad weather conditions of the first half of the 1970s because of the long-term trends already discussed.) Furthermore, the latest five-year plan (for 1976—1980) foresees an increase in per capita real income which is even slightly lower than the claimed achievement during 1971—1975. Given the central importance of steadily increasing consumption levels in the outlook of the Soviet public and in its assessment of the Party's leadership, and given the leaders' awareness of the public's attitude, the leveling off of the per capita consumption curve after 1970 is a phenomenon of great political importance. Coming as it does at a time of serious retardation in the expansion of the economy's resources and of uncertainty in the evolution of détente, it may well have appreciable bearing on the foreign as well as domestic policies of the USSR.

Plans for 1980 and 1990

It is in this setting that the USSR has embarked on its Tenth Five-Year Plan (1976—1980). The "Basic Directions" for the plan are fairly similar in length and format to the corresponding document for the Ninth plan (the "Directives" published in April 1971).[23] They are equally sparse in quantitative data. Possibly, in a year or so a book-length version will appear, as in the case of the Ninth plan, and we shall then know more of what is in store for the USSR in 1980. In the meantime, a later version of the Tenth plan has been confirmed by the CPSU Central Committee and the Supreme Soviet (see *Pravda*, October 26—30, 1976), though only a few figures have been revealed on this later occasion. These figures are generally the same—or fall within the same ranges—as those in the "Basic Directions."

In the postwar period, Soviet five-year plans have customarily been heralded by quite brief and ostensibly tentative documents such as the present "Basic Directions," and only in the case of the Ninth plan were they followed by the publication of a more or less comprehensive, book-length document. There is some reason to think that in most or all cases before 1972 no final version was published simply because no agreed-upon comprehensive plan was completed, although this fact was never publicly admitted.[24] If so, how do we interpret the role of medium-term plans in Soviet economic development? What does the Soviet Union's claim that its economy develops according to five-year plans really amount to if, in fact, between 1934 and 1972 few (if any) comprehensive plans were drawn up? Moreover, major new programs and revisions of old ones are frequently adopted in the course of the quinquennial period. What then is the meaning of five-year plans being fulfilled or not being fulfilled?

The marvel is not that Soviet medium-term plans are not fully drawn up but that the job is attempted at all, for it is basically an infeasible one, given the degree of detail and rigidity that the Soviet authorities require. The job takes several years, in the course of which the statistical base for planning needs continual updating, the whole world is changing, the leadership's goals and priorities are shifting, and sometimes the leadership itself changes. (Whether the job can be significantly speeded up and qualitatively improved with modern data processing equipment remains to be seen.) Even after the initial "guidelines" or "basic directions" are adopted by the CPSU Congress, it must still be very difficult, if not impossible, to produce within a reasonable time a comprehensive document that will be at once internally consistent and not out of tune with both reality and the leadership's priorities of the given moment. At the congress, Kosygin spoke quite frankly on this score. The 1972 publication of a book-length version of the Ninth plan is a good case in point: it was already partly obsolete the very moment it came off the press owing to the major crop failure of that year. And one wonders how good the "Basic Directions" for the Tenth plan are, considering that they must have been hastily revised because of the latest crop failure.

If it is very difficult to draw up a comprehensive, complete five-year plan, it is that much more difficult, in some respects, to draw up a fifteen-year plan. Therefore, one is hardly surprised to find that the "Basic Directions" fail even to mention the fifteen-year plan for 1976–1990 that has been under intensive concurrent preparation. The record of Soviet long-term plans (fifteen-year or twenty-year plans) is not a happy one. Although repeatedly attempted since the late 1920s, they have generally suffered from excessive optimism and minimal longevity. The latest—and most highly publicized—such attempt was Khrushchev's "Twenty-Year Program" for 1961–1980, announced in October 1961,[25] at the apogee of his post-Sputnik optimism. The program was to bring Soviet society to the threshold of full communism, that is, material abundance. Although its published targets were only global and very general and pertained only to the years 1970 and 1980, its lack of realism insured its being officially forgotten even before Khrushchev stepped out of power three years later. It is perhaps of some interest to compare the Tenth plan's targets for 1980 with those of Khrushchev's twenty-year program for the same year; such a comparison is provided in Table 5, where the figures are ratios (expressed as a per cent) of targets in the Tenth plan to those of the program. Where the available targets are in the form of ranges, the ratios employ midpoint values. Items in the top portion of the table—comparing the index series—may be overstated owing to the probable price inflation occurring between 1960 and 1975 (when the Tenth plan was compiled).

But to return to Brezhnev's fifteen-year program: referring to it as "guidelines" rather than as a plan, the General Secretary devoted a fair amount of time to it in his address to the Twenty-Fifth Congress. He observed that fifteen-year guidelines are not of a directive nature nor as detailed as five-year plans. Rather, their goal is "to determine the nature and size of the tasks facing [the USSR] in good time and to concentrate efforts on solving them; to have a clearer view of problems and difficulties; to facilitate the working out and fulfillment of programs and projects beyond the framework of one five-year period." Noting that

TABLE 5

THE YEAR 1980: A REVISED PROGNOSIS

(in percent, ratios of Tenth FYP targets to those
in Khrushchev's Twenty-Year Program)

Index Series			
National income	65	Coal	68
Industrial output	70	Cement	62
Producer goods	70	Mineral fertilizer	110
Consumer goods	72	Plastic and synthetic resins	29
Machine building	79	Synthetic fibers	46
Agricultural output[a]	50	Fabrics, altogether	61
Labor productivity in industry	71	Grain	78
Physical output series		Meat (slaughter weight)	49
		Milk	54
Electricity	48	Eggs	53
Ingot steel	67	Raw cotton	86
Crude oil	91	Sugar beets	94
Natural gas	62		

SOURCES: *Pravda*, October 18, 1961, and March 7, 1976.

[a]In the calculation of this ratio, the numerator was first derived by computing the percent increase between total output for the five-year period ending in 1950 and total output planned for the five-year period ending in 1980.

there "is still a great deal of work to be done on the concrete figures and tasks for the future," Brezhnev predicted that during 1976–1990 the USSR would "have at its disposal approximately twice as many material and financial resources as in the last fifteen-year period," as compared with an approximately 2.4-fold increase "in the volume of material goods and services" in the preceding fifteen years.[26] No other figures were mentioned. Although such grandiose visions have a certain propaganda value both at home and abroad, one suspects that the 1976–1990 plan, if ever completed, will soon join its predecessors in the archives of the State Planning Committee.

A Restrained Five-Year Plan

Returning to the Tenth Five-Year Plan, we first note that in terms of targeted growth rates, it is by far the most modest medium-term plan in Soviet history—a reflection of both long-term retardation in the growth of the Soviet economy and of the 1975 agricultural disaster.

The restraint in the plan is clearly evident if we compare the targets for 1976–1980 with those planned for 1971–1975 and the results annually achieved in that five-year period (see Table 3).[27] Thus the 1980 goal for national income utilized is set at a level 26 per cent higher than that of 1975, compared to a 38.6 per cent planned gain and a 28 per cent gain reportedly achieved from 1970 to 1975. For total industrial output, the corresponding figures are 36, 47, and 43 per cent; for output of industrial consumer goods (Group "B")—32, 48.6, and 37 per cent; for output of producer goods (Group "A," admittedly a catchall category of limited analytical significance)—38, 46.3, and 46 per cent; for agricultural output (measured by averages of annual output for the quinquennia ending in 1980 and 1975, respectively)—16, 23, and 13 per cent; for gross fixed investment (total value for the whole five-year periods)—26, 41.6, and 42 per cent;[28] and lastly, value of retail sales (state and cooperative)—28.7, 41.8, and 35 per cent.

The general picture of retardation that emerges from these global magnitudes is also confirmed by such detail as has been revealed to date. While especially marked in regard to personal consumption, it is also quite evident in several basic industries and in some machinery items. Thus the targets provide for the following percentage increases in the output of energy and basic materials during the Tenth plan period (for

comparison, officially claimed increases during the Ninth plan are shown
in parentheses):

Energy and Basic Materials	Targeted Percentage Increases
Electricity	33 (40)
Crude petroleum	30 (39)
Natural gas	50 (46)
Coal	15 (12)[29]
Ingot steel	19 (22)
Rolled steel (finished)	19 (22)
Nonferrous metals industry	26 (36)[30]
Mineral fertilizers	60 (63)
Synthetic resins and plastics	102 (67)
Synthetic fibers	53 (53)
Cement	18-21 (28)
Paper and paperboard	15-25 (28)

Although the figures show a high target for plastic and synthetic resins
relative to achieved growth in the previous plan period and indicate an
intention to maintain approximately the same rates of output growth as
in recent years for mineral fertilizers and synthetic fibers, it seems overall
that even if the respective 1980 targets are attained, growth in the total
supply of energy and basic materials will have slowed appreciably.

Among major industrial branches, chemicals and petrochemicals lead
the pack with a combined increase of 63 per cent. As for machine
building and metalworking, the target is to increase output by 1980 to 53
per cent over 1975, which is to be compared with the planned increase of
72 per cent for the previous five-year plan, and an actual increase
(apparently for machine building alone) of 73 per cent—a claim that, as
already noted, we have found difficult to substantiate. For the few
specific groups of machinery for which Tenth plan data are given, the
targeted percentage increases (and, in parentheses, claimed increases
during the 1971−1975 period) are as follows:[31]

Machinery	Targeted Percentage Increases
Automation equipment	60-70 (80)
Computer equipment and accessories	80 (330)[32]
Trucks (number)	15-19 (33)
Tractors (number)	6-10 (20)
Equipment for the light and food industries	30-40 (50)

It may be inferred[33] that the number of passenger automobiles to be produced in 1980 has been set at 1.2–1.3 million, at best a modest increase over the 1.2 million that were produced in 1975. Considering the lag of facilities behind the growing numbers of passenger cars and the high value that now attaches to the petroleum products burned by them, as well as the current intensification of Soviet efforts to export cars, particularly to the West, it seems quite likely that the number of passenger cars retained for domestic uses will not increase significantly over the next five years.[34]

Beyond the restraint evident in the Tenth Five-Year Plan targets, there are signs of a simultaneous and seemingly long-term shift of emphasis in favor of heavy industry. As Brezhnev said at the congress, "The main thrust of the Party's economic strategy that runs through both [!] the Tenth Five-Year Plan and the long-term [i.e., fifteen-year] program is further augmentation of the economic might of the country, expansion and radical modernization of production capacity, and insuring of stable and balanced growth for heavy industry, the foundation of our economy." The statement is printed in boldface. Missing from it is any explicit reference—standard in such contexts in recent years—to raising consumer welfare (though the theme is stressed in relation to the long-term program in a separate context).

However, even the reaffirmed priority of heavy industry apparently cannot forestall a sharp drop in the rate of increase of gross fixed investment[35]—a 26 percent increase in the Tenth plan against 42–45 per cent increases claimed in the three preceding quinquennia (though these claims may be overstated because of cost inflation). Evidently, the Soviet economy is entering a new historical phase when retardation in the rate of expansion of the capital stock interacts with the slowing in the growth of employment to force adjustment to a more modest pace of development.[36] It will be interesting to watch how consumption and defense fare in the squeeze.

Slower Improvement for Consumers

It is clear that the Tenth Five-Year Plan is no "consumers' plan" and not much claim is made that it is. (The Ninth was proclaimed to be one but was not.) By Soviet standards, the promises held out to consumers are rather modest in relation not only to earlier plans but even to past achievements, especially those in the first half of the Brezhnev-Kosygin leadership's tenure in office. For instance, real income per capita is to increase some 21 per cent by 1980, compared with claimed growth of 24 per cent during 1971–1975 and 33 per cent during 1966–1970. The average money wage/salary is to go up 17 per cent, compared with 20 and 26 per cent, respectively, claimed for earlier quinquennia. For collective farmers, the outlook appears better—a 26 per cent gain in income from the socialist sector—until one recalls that the base of the increase is 1975.

Turning to goods and services for the consumer, we also discover a moderating trend in growth. The Tenth plan promises an increase of 29 per cent in the level of retail sales, compared with the claimed 36 per cent in 1971–1975. The figures on the production side are quite consistent with this target. Thus output of light industry (mainly textiles, clothing, and footwear) is planned to rise by 27 per cent; durable consumer goods by 56.5 per cent; the food-processing industry by 24 per cent; meat and dairy products by 20–22 per cent; and fish and fish products for human consumption by 30–32 per cent.[37] Everyday services to the public (still a neglected area) are to increase in sales volume by 49 per cent, compared with a claimed 60 per cent during the Ninth Five-Year Plan.

Of particular importance to consumption is the expected lowering of sights in the Tenth Five-Year Plan for agriculture, where the gross value of average annual output during 1976–1980 is planned to increase 16 per cent, compared with a 23 per cent planned increase for 1971–1975 (and a 13 per cent achieved increase for that period). However, grain output is targeted at the high figure of 235 million tons for 1980, compared with an average of 191.9 million tons per year for 1971 through 1974—that is, excluding the small 1975 crop. How do these production targets translate into expected government procurements (which roughly approximate the food and technical-crop resources that are expected to be at the authorities' disposal)? Examining the procurement data in Table 6 (page 72), where the targets for 1980 are again presented as annual averages for 1976—1980, we discern a fairly clear pattern. The Tenth plan envisages the same absolute amounts of procurement of most chief field crops and animal products as did the Ninth plan for 1975—that is, for the terminal year of the 1971—1975 quinquennium.[38] Assuming that the planned average annual level of procurements will be reached in 1978, the midpoint of the 1976—1980 period, we see that the date for achieving the levels of procurement originally targeted for 1975 has been postponed for three years. These trends in procurement should be compared with a projected growth of almost 1 per cent per year for the total population and of nearly 2.5 per cent per year for the urban population.[39]

The target for procurement of livestock (including poultry) is of particular interest because of the high political importance that attaches to the satisfaction of demand for meat. According to the "Basic Directions," the average annual procurement of meat during 1976—1980 is set at 17.4 million tons or 13 per cent above the average during 1971—1975. This procurement compares with an increase of 33 per cent in the preceding quinquennium (1971—1975 in relation to 1966—1970) and 35 per cent in the one before (1966—1970 in relation to 1961—1965). The average annual growth of livestock procurement was therefore 6.0 per cent over the three quinquennia.[40] Over the same period, total money incomes are said to have increased by 113 per cent,[41] or 7.9 per cent per year on the average. The economist's income elasticity of demand for meat thus roughly works out to as much as 0.76 (6.0 ÷ 7.9), despite the sharp increase in official meat prices in 1962. Therefore, a 13 per cent increase in livestock procurement during the Tenth plan would seem to suffice to meet only a 17 per cent (13 ÷ 0.76) increase in total money incomes. Yet an increase in money incomes of no less than 30 per cent appears to be expected.[42] (At the same time, of course, there is no assurance that the planned increase in livestock procurement will actually materialize.) One wonders whether there will not be a serious aggravation of meat shortages in official stores, a substantial increase in official

TABLE 6

ANNUAL AGRICULTURAL PRODUCTION AND PROCUREMENTS 1971–1980

(millions of metric tons, except as noted)

	Ninth FYP		1975 Only		Tenth FYP
	1971-1975 Plan[a]	1971-1975 Actual[a]	Plan[b]	Actual	1976-1980 Plan[a]
Production					
Grain	195	181.5	214	140	215-20g
Potatoes	105.7	89.7	111.2	88.5	n.a.
Sunflower seed	7.0	6.0	7.4	5	7.6
Sugar beets	87.4	(76.4)[c]	92.4	66.5	95-98
Raw cotton	6.75	7.7	7.2	7.9	8.5
Flax fiber, 1000 tons	n.a.	454	556	478	540[f]
Vegetables	24.7	22	27.2	22d	n.a.
Meat (slaughter weight)	14.3	14	16.0	15.2	15-15.6
Milk	92.3	87.4	100.2	90.8	94-96
Eggs, billions	46.7	49.8	52.7	57.7	58-61
Wool (greasy), 1000 tons	464	441	500	463	n.a.
Procurements					
Grain	81	(72)	87	50.2	90
Potatoes	n.a.	(12.3)	16	14.6	16.8
Sunflower seed	5.7	(4.7)	5.9	3.8	6
Sugar beets	82	(69.2)	87	61.9	89.5
Raw cotton	6.8	(7.6)	7.2	7.9	8.5

TABLE 6 (Cont.)

ANNUAL AGRICULTURAL PRODUCTION AND PROCUREMENTS 1971–1980

(millions of metric tons, except as noted)

| | Ninth FYP | | 1975 Only | | Tenth FYP |
	1971-1975 Plan[a]	1971-1975 Actual[a]	Plan[b]	Actual	1976-1980 Plan[a]
Flax fiber, 1000 tons	n.a.	(414.5)	540	460.2	511
Vegetables	13.5	(12.9)	16	13.9	17
Fruit and berries	4.2	(3.6)	5.5	4.2	5.6
Grapes	4.6	(3.2)	5.4	4.3	5.4
Tea (leaves), 1000 tons	n.a.	(301.5)	303	352	n.a.
Livestock (including fowl), live weight	15.4	(15)	17.7	16.7	17.4
Milk	53.8	(51.1)	60.1	56.3	60.5
Eggs, billions	23.9	(26.1)	28.7	33.1	34.3
Wool (recorded weight), 1000 tons[e]	481	n.a.	520.6	n.a.	511

SOURCES: For 1971–1974 data, see *SSSR v tsifrakh v 1974 g.*; for 1975 data, *SSSR v tsifrakh v 1975 gg.*; for 1971–1975 and 1975 planned data, "1971–1975 Plan," see note 9 for Grossman/Chapter Five; for 1976–1980 planned data, see note 1 for Grossman/Chapter Five. Also see Karl-Eugen Wädekin, "Die sowjetische Landwirtschaft an der Wende zweier Planjahrfünfte," Bundesinstitut für ostwissenschaftliche und internationale Studien, *Bericht*e, no. 15, 1976).

NOTES: Where *n.a.* is indicated, figures were not available.

[a] Average amount per year.

[b] As targeted in the Ninth FYP. The 1975 annual plan set revised production targets, in most cases differing only slightly from the Ninth FYP targets for the year. However, some of the revised targets should be mentioned: grain–215.7 million tons; cotton–7.7 million tons; meat–15.3 million tons; milk–94.8 million tons; eggs–53.3 billion; and wool–472 million tons.

[c] Production and procurement figures in parentheses are average annual data for 1971–1974 only.

[d] 1975 output of vegetables was "approximately on the average yearly level of the Ninth FYP."

[e] These figures should not be compared with the wool production figures above.

[f] As estimated by Dr. Wädekin.

[g] 235 targeted for 1980 (*Pravda*, October 28, 1976, p. 2).

management efficiency perhaps to a greater degree than even the Ninth plan. Yet one may be somewhat skeptical of planner optimism in this regard, particularly because there seem to be no signs of major economic reform forthcoming.

In regard to resources, we have already noted the further retardation in the rate of growth of industrial employment (less than 1 per cent per year implied for 1976–1980, compared with 1.3 per cent per year achieved during 1971–1975), and there is a clear suggestion of an absolute decline in rural manpower.[45] The pace of fixed-capital accumulation will probably slow even more substantially, given the already mentioned reduction in the rates of increase of fixed investment and of the output of investment goods. The expectation that fixed capital stock in industry will nonetheless increase by as much as 40 per cent (compared with an estimated 47 per cent in 1971–1975) is seemingly accounted for by a renewed determination to channel investment funds on a priority basis to projects nearest completion. In the past, repeated attempts to pursue such a policy did not stick.

Insofar as the operating methods by which the Soviet leadership hopes to achieve such striking gains in efficiency are concerned, it is clear that the economy is to stay firmly on essentially the same institutional course and to continue the trends of the past five years. No significant economic reform—in the sense of liberalization or decentralization—is suggested. The 1965 reform is not even recalled in either the "Basic Directions" or the two leading addresses before the congress, those of Brezhnev and Kosygin. Indeed, the majority of measures spelled out in these sources will, if anything, insure continued retreat from the reform. Among such measures are: further emphasis on the creation of large-scale production units ("associations," "territorial complexes") not only in industry but also in construction and in agriculture (including some vertical integration between industry and agriculture); tighter planning of the use and distribution of producer goods; firmer application of labor-productivity standards; a continued search for better methods of central planning and other means of improving the existing system;[46] and more rigid delivery quotas for agriculture. Great emphasis is placed on the computerization of planning and management.

In view of all this, Brezhnev's call for greater attention to prices and profits in business decisions does not have the ring that it might convey if taken by itself. The greater leeway of managerial action it seems to imply will quickly run up against the strengthened administrative controls.

Of some interest is the proposal — particularly emphasized by

Kosygin—to improve planning by means of "integral programs" (*kompleksnye programmy*) for the solution of key problems that cut across administrative boundaries. The formation of an industrial base for the development of atomic power was mentioned by him in this connection. The idea is not new: the Soviet nuclear-weapons and space programs must have been managed in this fashion; their strength and weakness at once lie in the fact that they cut across the administrative grain of the economy and are free of the fetters and vested interests of existing bureaucratic structures. At the same time, they interfere with the routine functioning of the system as a whole. It will be interesting to see whether new "integral programs" are launched in the near future, and what their success will be.

Quite consistently, in light of the pressure on resources and the unfavorable prospects for the growth of consumer goods and services, the "Basic Directions" also contain repeated reaffirmations of the principle of material incentives, that is, reliance on the pay envelope to bring out better performance by all and sundry in the economy. "Rubles for work" has been the dominant approach in recent years, despite lip service to moral incentives and socialist competition. The implications of this emphasis, of course, spill over beyond the production sphere into various social and ideological realms which do not concern us here.

The Tenth Five-Year Plan is being publicized as the "five-year plan of efficiency and quality," meaning that the quality and technical modernity of manufactured articles are to receive much greater attention than heretofore. Mandatory industrial standards are being tightened, while at the same time a larger carrot is proffered through more flexible pricing of new products and the offer of monetary incentives to individuals who develop and produce improved products and raise quality.[47] Yet it is difficult to see how a major jump in terms of product quality and modernity can take place while the established economic institutions and policies that have had so much to do with unsatisfactory performance are being reaffirmed and reinforced.

The "Basic Directions" call for measures to "increase the role of foreign economic relations in solving economic problems and accelerating scientific and technical progress" during 1976–1980. Both Brezhnev and Kosygin elaborated on this general theme. Brezhnev especially emphasized, at length, the policy of ever-closer economic integration with the other members of CMEA—interestingly, doing so within the context of his discussion of political relations with the other socialist countries rather than in the section of his address dealing with foreign trade. Both he and Kosygin looked forward to a greater variety of forms of business relations with Western firms, and both stressed barter ("product-payback") arrangements, hoping that such arrangements will encompass more than just the traditional Soviet export commodities. Kosygin particularly emphasized the need for more effective organization of the Soviet export industries.

These policies in the realm of foreign economic relations are, of course, quite consistent with the outlook for the Soviet economy generally. The overall retardation of the economy, together with persistent lags in the mastering of modern technology (a problem that also received attention at the Twenty-Fifth Congress), combined with continued heavy claims against the country's resources, argue for seeking external help "in solving economic problems" (in the just cited words of the "Basic Directions"). But the rising role of debt service in the Soviet hard-currency account prompts caution—hence the stress on product-payback arrangements with Western firms. These can lighten the balance-of-payments problems in the future (and, incidentally, can be later turned into levers of political pressure on Western firms and their governments, as well).[48]

Summing Up

At this point, midway through the 1970s, the Soviet economy is showing distinct signs of aging. Though still increasing by most standards, economic growth slowed significantly during the Ninth plan period, and that plan's ambitious targets were generally missed (sometimes widely) as a result of the decline in labor reserves and other retardatory forces and the impact of two major crop failures. Agricultural production was particularly hard hit; consumer goods output and consumption levels rose much less than planned; and civilian equipment production and capital formation also fell short of expectations. Nonetheless, Soviet heavy industrial output expanded at high rates, and presumably military production did well too. Moreover, the recession in the West made the historically modest Soviet industrial performance look particularly good.

The Tenth Five-Year Plan (1976–1980) envisages further retardation of growth throughout the economy. The advance in consumption levels is expected to slow down even further; and fixed investment and capital formation will be slow. Labor productivity, although relied on heavily to promote growth, will also rise more slowly. Despite the relative moderation of the plan's goals, they may still turn out to be rather ambitious in relation to resources. No liberalizing reforms seem to be in the offing; rather, there is strong emphasis on centralism in planning and management, with further mergers of enterprises into rather large units and computerization. Still, the industrial basis of Soviet power—including military might—will certainly continue to grow at a pace that would be creditable for any advanced industrial power.

The longer term slowing down of overall growth, and especially of consumption, together with mounting pressures on resources from a variety of domestic quarters and the refractory problems of bridging the "technology gap," nevertheless make certain that the Soviet leadership will be faced with many difficult choices of both a political and an economic nature. Hence, to this observer, it seems most likely that the middle-aged USSR economy will continue to seek a "boost" from the West in the form of credits, goods, and technology—something that could work to the West's diplomatic advantage.

chapter six / *Roman Kolkowicz*

The Military in Soviet Politics: From the Perspective of the Twenty-Fifth Party Congress

The proceedings of the Twenty-Fifth Congress of the CPSU convey a somewhat distorted picture of the military's role in Soviet politics and society at large. On the face of it, the military's role at the congress was modest and subdued; there was little of the usual sabre or missile rattling by military speakers; the traditional report by a leading military figure to the congress was omitted altogether; the military's top representative in the Party's ruling bodies (the Politburo and the Central Committee) was not a military professional but a civilian, the new Minister of Defense, Dmitrii Ustinov; and finally, the proportional representation of the military in the newly elected Central Committee was somewhat reduced by the Party leadership. These factors and others may lead some foreign analysts to the conclusion that the role of the Soviet military has been curtailed by the Brezhnev leadership and that, far from remaining a strong and autonomy-seeking institution, the military has in fact become a pliable tool of Party politics.

It is my contention that these developments do not indicate any reduction in the military's basic institutional and political role. I would argue instead that the institutional strength of the military in the Soviet Union remains firm and may possibly be increasing, and that it continues to play an important but tacit role in the affairs of the state and the Party. To properly perceive the strength of the military in Soviet politics, one needs a broader historical perspective; it is my assumption that the military's steady and incremental institutional and political growth is a function of a number of developments in the Soviet system. In other words, the flow of Party-military relations and the relative strength of the latter vis-à-vis the former are influenced by certain evolutionary changes in Party and state.

The Dynamics of Party-Military Relations

It is my hypothesis that in many communist countries the armed forces are gradually assuming an important and increasingly autonomous role in the political process. My analytical framework, therefore, focuses on the interplay of several factors which, over recent decades, have resulted in a cumulative growth of the role of the military. This hypothesis is based upon three considerations.

1. Civil-military relations in the Soviet Union are shaped by important systemic, structural, and ideological parameters which provide the "rules of the game" for their interaction:

(a) Hegemonial power of the single party
(b) The absence of constitutional, legal, or traditional provisions for the transfer of political power in the Party and thus effectively in the state
(c) The presence of security organs and paramilitary organizations within and around the military establishment
(d) The anti-militaristic traditions of Marxism-Leninism which considered standing professional armies to be an implicit threat to the revolutionary goals and Party hegemony in communist societies

These factors have served as parametric constraints that have shaped and contained civil-military relations over the years. They have generated both a sense of distrust by Party leaders of the military professionals and their strong dependence on the military's skills for the defense of the country and the Party.

2. The "rules of the game," to which I referred, specified an unchallenged formal primacy of the Party in all affairs of the state, including the military; the need to retain strong and effective control mechanisms in the military *via* political control organs; the use of terror instruments and paramilitary organizations separate from the military structure; an institutionalized distrust of the military's values and intentions, particularly at times of intra-Party crises created by succession problems, internecine Party struggles, or threats from outside.

These constraints were imposed early on in Soviet history. However, as the nature of the Soviet political system evolved and was transformed, and as its domestic and foreign objectives and priorities underwent change, so did the relationship between the Party and the military. These changes have been influenced by several salient variables.

(a) The level of political development
(b) The level of economic development
(c) The mode and scope of the Party's authority and leadership
(d) The level of influence of countervailing security and paramilitary organs
(e) The scope and levels of commitment of foreign and defense policies

The basic conceptual approaches of Western analysts studying the military's roles in various political systems vary sharply according to the locus of the country in one of three geographic zones under analysis. These three areas were assumed to contain, respectively: societies undergoing gradual, evolutionary change in the *developed* world; societies undergoing rapid, almost revolutionary change, or where conditions for such change are assumed to be imminent in the *developing* or Third World; and societies which are assumed to remain politically static, while technologically and economically modernizing at a rapid rate, in the *communist* world. Correspondingly, the military in developed societies is not considered an important instrument of change; in developing societies, it is considered an important (actual or potential) source of change; and in communist societies, the military's capabilities or willingness to effect change has rarely, if ever, been considered.

There are many reasons for this last assumption among Western analysts. Aside from such obvious ones as absence of reliable data and access, an important reason derives from a confusion about the relations between the military and political authorities in communist systems.

Western social scientists generally assume that the process of political and economic modernization depends on certain necessary conditions, and that modernization produces certain predictable results. The essential conditions for modernization usually include a rational approach to decision making, a general secularization of sociopolitical values, and a modicum of institutional-functional autonomy of vital subgroups in society. Among the postulated consequences of modernization are greater efficiency, enhanced standards of living, and greater participation of citizens and groups in the political processes of the state. In attempting to apply these concepts to communist societies, analysts quickly encountered massive problems. At the root of their quandary was the inability to square the empirical reality of rapid economic-technological change and development in the "totalitarian" communist system with the virtual reversal of anticipated consequences of such rapid modernization. Therefore, the conclusion emerged that either the Western modernization models were wrong or inapplicable or, alternatively, that the communist systems were different from others, being *sui generis*.

The conceptual problematics derived from the persistence of two basic Western concepts of modernization which revolve around the *sequential* progression of economic and political development. One is a unilinear concept, an almost sequential process of nation building, in which political development follows upon economic development, suggesting that only in economically developed societies can political institutions exist and thrive. In subscribing to such a sequential model of development, analysts perceived the actual or potential roles of the military to be of great importance in "developing" societies. The military was analyzed in terms of its role as a *vehicle* or *accelerator* of economic and political development.

A more recent approach to modernization suggested a reversible model, indicating the possibility of economic development *and* retardation or retrogression of political development under conditions where modernization proceeds at a very rapid pace. Here the military is seen as an *impediment* to political development.

In the study of communist societies—specifically, the Soviet Union—one may want to introduce a third approach. In the USSR (the dominant model for other communist systems) the Western developmental-modernizing model appears to have been placed on its head. The Soviet state began as a highly complex political and organizational structure imposed upon a relatively underdeveloped economic substructure. Most of the conditions generally associated in the West with political development were present such as high political participation, intensive political socialization, effective national integration, "rational" decision making, and bureaucratic management. Yet this vast politically "developed" apparatus rested on a backward economic substructure, an inheritance of imperial ineptitude, mismanagement, and wartime devastation.

The Soviet leaders reversed the assumed sequential process of economic development preceding political development. For a central purpose of these imposed, "developed" political structures and processes was to accelerate economic development, technological innovation, urbanization, and the like. To be sure, it can be argued that much of this so-called "political development" and these advanced structures and processes remained merely symbolic, empty of content; that the "totalitarian" ruler and his supportive elites were engaged in meaningless duplications of "democratic" forms. Yet we cannot dismiss the fact that formally many of the processes associated with nation building and modernization were present at a very early stage in the history of the Soviet Union.

Thus, in attempting to analyze the role of the military in communist systems and to relate it to the modernization process within such states, we must employ approaches and methods other than those generally used by Western analysts for the study of the military in "developed" or "developing" societies. Moreover, the role of the military, again in an idiosyncratic manner, grew and developed with the progress in economic development *and* political retrogression from the developed "totalitarian" model. In this manner, the role of the military in the Soviet Union has followed a somewhat different pattern from that in most "developed" or "developing" countries.

Now, if the changing levels of political or economic development in the Soviet Union suggest an enhanced institutional and political role for the military, so do the three other principal factors from the list under item 2: (c) The changes in the mode and scope of Party leadership (going from a dictatorial, one-man Stalinist *vozhd'* model to one of "collective leadership" and bureaucratic coalitions in the Politburo and Central Committee) have somewhat diluted the Party's tight hold on the military and correspondingly enhanced the input and influence of the latter on the Party leadership. (d) The reduced role of the security apparatus, the traditional "equalizer" of the Stalinist system, has correspondingly enhanced the military's institutional health and influence. (e) And, finally, the enormously increased scope of Soviet political, diplomatic, and military involvement around the globe has given a correspondingly increased role to the military.

Consequently, it is possible to suggest that the level of the military's institutional and political strength in the Soviet Union is *inversely* proportional to the level of influence of countervailing security and paramilitary organs and the scope of the Party's authority and mode of leadership; at the same time, military strength is *directly* proportional to the levels of economic development and the scope and level of commitment of Soviet foreign and defense policies.

3. The interplay of these five factors over the past six decades has resulted in significant changes in civil-military relations in the Soviet Union. The history of civil-military relations suggests, moreover, that the role of the military and its institutional strength vis-à-vis the Party have been strongly affected by some systemic changes in the Soviet state and changes in the main direction of societal priorities over the years. The three main phases in the development of the system are:

(a) A period of intense national-political *integration* of the Soviet state, approximately during the Stalin period
(b) A period of political-economic *transformation* of the Soviet system, from the Stalinist-totalitarian type to one more participatory, less coercive, and less "beleaguered," approximating the Khrushchev period
(c) The contemporary period of political, economic, and military *expansionism* of Soviet politics, corresponding to the Brezhnev regime

In studying these major phases of the Soviet system, one also perceives roughly corresponding modes of Party-military relations:

(a) An initial phase of the military's *subordination* to the Party
(b) A subsequent phase of political *cooptation* of military elites by the Party into vital decision-making bodies and structures
(c) The current phase of mutual *accommodation* between the Party and the military elites

Each of these phases in civil-military relations corresponds to the major transformations in the general political development of the Soviet system, going from a revolutionary society to the present superpower status. Thus one may roughly relate the two:

(a) An initial phase of military subordination coincided with the process of intensive national-political integration of the state
(b) The period of military cooptation coincided with the political-economic transformation of the Soviet system
(c) The current period of mutual accommodation between the Party and the military corresponds to the political and military expansionism of Soviet politics

It is suggested, therefore, that the institutional and political role of the military in the Soviet Union is a function of internal and political modernization, with the corresponding complexity of decision making and stronger policy inputs by functional elites; it is a function of changes in the mode and scope of Party leadership within the state, thus permitting a stronger participatory role of vital bureaucratic elites within the Party; it is a function of the vastly expanding scope of Soviet commitments around the globe. Thus the process and phase of Party-military accommodation logically and empirically fit the present structure of Soviet domestic and foreign policy.

Party-Military Accommodation

The rather subdued role of the military at the Twenty-Fifth Party Congress suggests, at least to this writer, not military disadvantage or weakness but rather a sense of institutional vigor and self-assurance. It also suggests the Party's need (and the military's acquiescence) to enhance its public posture of détente and the avoidance of harsh, military posturing.

The military's basic institutional interests have been essentially satisfied by the Brezhnev regime:

- The budgetary allocations for the defense sector continue at high and steady levels
- The size of the armed forces, in terms of sheer manpower, has risen to over four million
- Defense-related R & D programs and the modernization and upgrading programs of the Strategic Forces, Navy, Air Force, and Theater Forces have continued unabated in recent years
- The military obtained, for the first time in many years, a seat on the Politburo in the person of Minister of Defense Marshal Grechko
- The military participates in a vigorous, at times dominant fashion in international negotiations, including SALT
- Military leaders have been entrusted by the Party with important political-diplomatic missions in Africa, the Middle East, and Asia, where they act as spokesmen for the Party
- The military is enjoying a Party-directed set of sociopolitical programs that aim at an intensive inculcation of martial values throughout the society, particularly in the educational system (a circumstance which has led Herbert Goldhammer, of the RAND Corporation, to conclude in a recent study that the Soviet Union is moving in the direction of a "nation in arms")

In the light of these institutional gains by the military, one need not be surprised that military leaders are publicly supportive of the Party's policies of détente and arms control. It has been frequently assumed in the West that any significant relaxation of tension on the international scene would threaten the military's rationale for high budgetary demands and top priority in social and economic planning. However, one of the ironies and paradoxes of modern détente, stable deterrence, and arms control policies, is that they have not only failed to slow down the massive arms programs—in the Soviet Union as elsewhere—but that they actually seem to propel and encourage both a qualitative and a quantitative arms-race spiral.

The military spokesmen can strike a peaceful pose, therefore, since they are assured that their basic institutional interests will continue to be satisfied by the Party leadership and that a constant influx of modern weapons technologies will continue to support the vastly increased Soviet political and military commitments. After all, the Party's activist and expanding commitments depend to an ever-growing degree on military support.

Conclusions and Projections

The Soviet military establishment participated in the Twenty-Fifth Party Congress amidst auspicious circumstances. Internally, the military was rather quiescent, unified, and generally satisfied with its institutional status, budgetary allocations, the influx of weapons and technology, and the freedom to manage its own affairs without excessive interference from the Party and its political control organs. Moreover, the military expanded its presence and influence globally, through its modern navy, military-space technology, strategic weapons systems, and increased presence in allied states in Africa, the Middle East, and Asia. The military challenged and overcame Khrushchev's policies of both defense economizing and military-political adventurism; now it enjoys a preferential position under the Brezhnev leadership.

The present favorable position of the military represents the culmination of a twenty-year trend of cumulative growth in institutional strength, corporate autonomy, professional sophistication, and political influence. What are the likely implications of this development?

The values and preferences of the military include a set of conservative social and political views. It prefers a society that is stable, fairly conservative, orderly, and committed to the ideas and objectives espoused by the Party. It generally views political deviancy, social experimentation, "liberalism," and excessive consumerism as antithetic to its own code of values, as well as detrimental to an orderly and disciplined society. The military prefers a national planning policy in which the security of the state receives the highest priority.

While the military is progressively more given to technocratic-managerial ways and values, it continues to retain the morale-building and corporative self-identifying values derived from the more heroic and revolutionary traditions and symbols of the Red Army.

The Soviet military and the current Party leadership seem to have reached a *modus vivendi,* a political and bureaucratic accommodation. It is likely to be sustained throughout this decade and into the next one, unless the premises of this accommodation are changed. In projecting Party-military relations into the future, we may want to extend the model of subordination, cooptation, and accommodation as successive stages, and consider alternative future modes of such relations.

We may wish to consider, above all, a militarization phase of civil-military relations and of Soviet politics in general. As the scope of Soviet foreign and defense policies increases, as the political and ideological dynamism of the Party elites abates, and as the bureaucratic-coalition form of governing becomes even more predominant, the military will find itself in a better position to assert its demands, priorities, and authority within the state. Such a trend would lead to a stronger influence of the military point of view in the leading Party organs and the governmental bureaucracies.

Alternatively, one might consider the likelihood of Party-military relations reverting to some earlier forms of military subordination or cooptation. Such a development would be contingent upon the emergence of a more conservative and ideologically more potent Party leadership, which would seek to curb the "excessive" growth of the military's institutional and political power as threatening to the Party. Or one might consider other alternative models that would assume different institutional and political circumstances.

My own preference lies with the militarization model of future Soviet Party-military relations, for several reasons. The Soviet military is essentially a conservative, nationalistic, Party-loyal institution whose members share most of the important objectives and values of the Party. The Party's growing reliance upon the military in the pursuit of ever-increasing, global Soviet foreign and military policies creates a marked dependence, or interdependence, between the Party leaders and the

military elites, thus enhancing the influence of military views and preferences. The persistence of collective leadership as a permanent coalition form of governance tends to reduce the Party's ability vigorously to
resist the concerted bureaucratic pressures of the vast military machine.

In the final analysis, however, the military is likely to remain a key
supportive actor in the Party's policies at home and abroad. It has a vital
stake in the present regime, in its policies, and in its good civil-military
relations. The Soviet Union as a superpower is likely to continue an
active and dynamic foreign policy, with interests and commitments
reaching far afield: the military's role in such a policy schema will remain
prominent and vital. Of the salient new developments—détente, active
international trade, the muting of the excesses of a neo-totalitarian
system, and Soviet willingness to enter into arms-limitation negotiations
and agreements—none negate or seriously invalidate our initial assumptions and argument.

Foreign Policy: The Soviet Union and the Noncommunist World

Perhaps the most striking characteristic of Brezhnev's treatment of Soviet relations with the noncommunist world, in his report to the Twenty-Fifth Congress of the CPSU, is its blandness. Both in his manner of presentation and in the substance of his speech, there is nothing that is new, dramatic, or controversial. However, a closer examination of Brezhnev's speech indicates that this is quite deliberate, and indeed it might be said that there is a method to his blandness.

In discussing relations with the noncommunist countries of the world, Brezhnev adopted a calm, pragmatic, and businesslike tone, one that is quite different from his speeches to the Twenty-Third and Twenty-Fourth Party Congresses. Thus we find that the ideological element has been reduced to a bare minimum, and the references to Lenin are few and far between. The main emphasis of the General Secretary's presentation is clearly on state-to-state relations with other governments and not on processes of class struggle and revolutionary transformation. Although the analogy should not be pushed too far, it can still be said that Brezhnev's speech reads more like the report of a foreign minister or prime minister than that of a Communist Party Secretary.

The departure from past practice is perhaps best illustrated by comparing the subheadings of the main sections of Brezhnev's speech with those of previous congresses. In the past, it was traditional to employ such subheadings as "Imperialism is the Enemy of the Peoples and of Social Progress" and "The Deepening of the Contradictions of the Capitalist System." In contrast, at the Twenty-Fifth Party Congress, the main section of Brezhnev's speech dealing with Soviet policy toward the noncommunist world was given the low-key, nonideological title of "The Development of Relations with the Capitalist States."

In keeping with this "businesslike" orientation, Brezhnev went out of his way to avoid using the term "American imperialism," and he barely mentioned that old whipping horse of Soviet propaganda, "German revanchism." Of course, this toning down of traditional Soviet vituperation might be attributable to the major improvement in Soviet relations with these two countries in recent years. But it should be noted that Brezhnev's speech also carefully avoided any attacks upon "Zionism," despite the continued absence of diplomatic relations with Israel (which were broken by the Soviet Union in 1967) and despite the incessant campaign against "Zionist intrigues" and "Israeli aggression" in the Soviet press.

In tone and style, then, it can be said that this is indeed a rather extraordinary speech. On the other hand, as far as matters of substance are concerned, Brezhnev's speech is rather unexceptional. There is no indication or even hint of a re-evaluation of past policies or the launching of new initiatives. Brezhnev's speech and the subsequent proceedings of the congress suggest that the Soviet Union will continue the same policies that it has pursued in the last several years in relation to détente, Soviet-American relations, the Middle East, China, and the Third World. Even in those areas where past Soviet initiatives have been completely barren of positive results (such as proposals for Asian collective security and multilateral security guarantees in the Middle East), Brezhnev calls for more of the same.[1]

Even those who are incurably addicted to kremlinological sleuthing will find little hint of any future shifts in the Soviet line, with one possible—though highly speculative—exception. The fact that Brezhnev avoids any attack on Zionism and states that the Soviet Union has "no prejudices" against any of the countries of the Middle East might be taken as a sign of possible Soviet willingness at least to consider the re-establishment of diplomatic relations with Israel. But in the absence of corroborative evidence, this remains pure conjecture.

In reporting on the most explosive and controversial areas of international politics, Brezhnev is careful to adopt a balanced, middle-of-the-road position. For example, in regard to détente we find no exaggerated claims or extravagant praise for the improvement in East-West relations that occurred since the last Party congress, but also no overt signs of Soviet disillusionment with détente and no inflammatory attacks on Western opponents of détente. As a shrewd and cautious politician, Brezhnev avoids unrealistic claims which might expose him to attack from his Politburo colleagues should East-West relations deteriorate, just as he eschews sharp criticism of Western critics of détente which would receive extensive publicity abroad and would provide further ammunition for those in the West who argue that Soviet hostility to the outside world continues unabated.

In this connection, it is noteworthy that Brezhnev's treatment of American foreign policy is especially restrained. He goes out of his way to avoid time-honored clichés critical of the U.S., and when he condemns American policies in Vietnam, Angola, and Chile, he assiduously avoids the phrase, "American imperialism." It is also significant that one of the very few instances in which the official record of the congress was tampered with so as to alter the sense of a delegate's comments was to *eliminate* a reference to American imperialism. Gaston Plissonier, the head of the French Communist Party delegation to the Twenty-Fifth Congress, in his speech of February 28, 1976, stated: "The French government has, in fact, put our country back into NATO, which is led by American imperialism."[2] When this speech was reported the following day in *Pravda,* the phrase, "which is led by American imperialism," was omitted.[3]

There is, then, no evidence of any modification of the Soviet interest in détente. Another indication of continuity in this area is provided by the further political advance of Georgii Arbatov, the director of the prestigious and highly influential Institute of United States and Canadian Studies. Arbatov, who has been closely associated with the present trend in Soviet-American relations, both as an adviser to Brezhnev and as a prominent public commentator on East-West relations, was promoted at the Twenty-Fifth Congress to candidate member of the Central Committee. (He had become a member of the Central Auditing Commission in 1971.)

The proceedings of the congress are quite barren of anything exciting concerning the national-liberation movements in the Third World. It is true that Brezhnev did explicitly reaffirm the basic line which states that détente, far from being a process that freezes and stabilizes the status quo, is in fact a means of creating the most favorable conditions for the success of the national-liberation struggle. Yet despite the exaggerated importance attached to this statement by some Western journalists, assertions such as these do not in any way represent a hardening of the Soviet position. Brezhnev's statement is a reiteration of the standard formula which has been put forth for almost two decades and which—it should be noted—has been directed mainly at rebutting the criticism of hardline elements within the communist world who advocate the abandonment of détente in favor of a more forceful struggle against "imperialism." Whatever actual Soviet beliefs may be about the true relation between détente and the national-liberation struggle, such a rhetorical stand is unavoidable in view of the Soviet search for Third World support and its advocacy of "proletarian internationalism." For this reason, Soviet claims of an intimate link between détente and the "world revolutionary process" can be considered neither edifying nor alarming.

A further example of the carefully modulated tone of Brezhnev's comments on foreign policy is his discussion of those areas in which the Soviet Union has experienced either significant successes or appreciable setbacks since the last congress. Brezhnev gives the Soviet Union a great deal of credit—perhaps more than merited—for the successes achieved in Indochina and Angola. Nevertheless, he is careful not to engage in any loud self-congratulation or boasting, which might produce a counterproductive reaction in the West. Similarly, in touching upon those areas where friction has developed between the Soviet Union and another country, Brezhnev studiously avoids—in a manner quite different from that of his predecessor—any harsh criticism which might serve to make an already delicate situation even worse.

In discussing Soviet-Japanese relations, Brezhnev attempts to put the best possible face on things by stating that these relations are "moving in a generally positive direction." There is no evidence in his remarks of any inclination to follow up on Foreign Minister Gromyko's warning of January 1976 that the Japanese decision to sign a peace treaty with China would have serious consequences for Soviet-Japanese relations.[4]

At the time of his major speech to the Twenty-Fifth Congress (February 24), Brezhnev was clearly unprepared for Egyptian President Anwar Sadat's repudiation, less than three weeks later, of the Treaty of Friendship and Cooperation between the two countries.[5] Sadat's action was unanticipated—as indicated by Brezhnev's reference to this treaty, which Egypt was soon to abrogate unilaterally, as "a long-term basis for relations in the interests of not only our countries but also the entire Arab world." Hoping to avoid a further deterioration of Soviet-Egyptian relations and apparently determined not to provoke it, Brezhnev went out of his way at the congress to avoid any personal criticism of Sadat.

In view of this overall approach to questions of foreign policy, it is not inaccurate to say that the whole area of Soviet relations with the noncommunist world was really a nonissue as far as the record of the Twenty-Fifth Congress was concerned. The situation was compounded by the fact that the Ministers of Foreign Affairs and Defense did not even speak at the Party congress this time. Apparently, this departure from past practice was primarily because of the central role of economic planning in the concerns of the congress. Most of the agenda was occupied by prosaic economic questions centering on the Tenth Five-Year Plan, and there was little reference to foreign policy questions in the speeches of the Soviet officials and foreign communist leaders who followed Brezhnev to the podium. Any overt controversy over foreign policy concerned relations within the communist camp, and revolved around such questions as the correct definition of proletarian internationalism, the degree of independence to be accorded foreign communist parties, and the role of a communist party in a democratic state. Here there was genuine disagreement, but there is no evidence in the record of the Party congress of any similar controversy concerning the Soviet Union's pursuit of détente or its conduct of relations with the noncommunist world.

Thus it can be said that Brezhnev's speech seeks to convey a degree of both satisfaction and caution in present Soviet foreign policy. There is indeed much reason for satisfaction since the international position of the Soviet Union has improved markedly during Brezhnev's stewardship over the past decade. Strategic parity with the United States has been achieved; the Soviet position in Eastern Europe has been strengthened and stabilized; the ideological and political challenge from China, which seemed very worrisome in the mid-1960s, has been blunted; the United States has been expelled from Indochina; and considerable success has been achieved in obtaining access to Western goods and technology.

Yet, at the same time, there is good reason for the Soviet leadership to temper this satisfaction with a large dose of caution. Brezhnev and his Politburo colleagues are well aware of the fragile nature of the existing equilibrium and of the ever-present danger of rapid and unpredictable change. Détente is under sharp criticism in the West. Relations between the Soviet Union and China remain explosive. There is no guarantee against future unrest in Eastern Europe. Soviet relations with Third World countries remain unpredictable and, especially in the Middle East, unsatisfactory. And the growing independence of major nonruling communist parties, such as the Italian and French, could in the future pose monumental problems which might even threaten the ideological legitimacy of Soviet control in Eastern Europe and perhaps within the Soviet Union itself.

At the Twenty-Fourth Party Congress in 1971, Brezhnev announced a broad range of Soviet initiatives to further détente. In contrast, the

Foreign Policy:
Communist States and Parties

There were more delegates from more countries at the Twenty-Fifth Congress of the CPSU than at any previous congress. According to TASS, 103 delegations from 96 countries represented communist, socialist, and liberation parties from around the world. The increase was not the result of new communist parties, though, according to Brezhnev, the international communist movement had grown by one million new members since the Twenty-Fourth Congress in 1971. Instead, the increase was accounted for by the presence of many delegations from noncommunist liberation movements, especially from Africa but also from the Middle East, many of which came to the congress on Soviet invitation for the first time.

Mikhail Suslov, the Politburo member charged with special responsibility for the international communist movement, said in his welcoming speech:

> There have never been so many fraternal delegations at one of our Party congresses. . . . This is evidence of the further expansion and strengthening of the life-giving bonds of internationalism which link our Party unbreakably with all the participants in the world-wide front of the struggle for peace and the freedom of the peoples and for social progress. The Party of Lenin carries high and will continue steadfastly to carry the sacred banner of proletarian internationalism.[1]

Similarly, in his major address, Brezhnev spoke at length and with feeling on the subject of proletarian internationalism, praising those who practice it and condemning those who repudiate it.

"Proletarian internationalism" is a handy euphemism, a shorthand symbol for Soviet leadership of the international communist movement. Everybody in the movement knows this meaning of the term. But were the many delegations attending the congress indeed evidence of the growth and strengthening of proletarian internationalism? Brezhnev and Suslov said that they were, dwelled on them, and stressed the large foreign contingent present at the congress at every opportunity. Hindsight suggests that the two Soviet leaders overemphasized the foreign connection precisely because they needed to bolster the Soviet claim to leadership of the movement. They had anticipated and feared that complications in this respect might take place during the Party congress. As it turned out, they were right.

Here Brezhnev and Suslov did not worry so much about China and Albania, whose representatives were absent from this congress, as they have been ever since 1962. Brezhnev did attack China, and it was a strong condemnation. He charged that China was attempting to wreck détente, to prevent disarmament, and to provoke a new cold war. But this was nothing new. And neither, after all, were the speeches of Nicolae Ceausescu of Rumania and Stane Dolanc of Yugoslavia (President Tito did not show up and sent Dolanc instead): as usual, both of them put emphasis on the equality of *all* parties and thus repudiated claims to Soviet superordination. Ceausescu called for "the right of every party independently to elaborate its own political life and revolutionary strategy and tactics," while Dolanc stressed "the principles of equality, independence, and responsibility of each movement towards its own working class and people." Again, these appeals were familiar—annoying to Moscow but not surprising and not intolerable.

Instead, Brezhnev and Suslov must have worried about the West European parties, especially the Italian and the French Communist Parties—the largest, most influential, and most important in the international communist movement—but also about the British, Belgian, Swedish, Spanish, and possibly other communist parties abroad. In fact, the Soviet leaders had anticipated problems with these parties for quite some time; there were many unmistakable signs indicating brewing disagreement between them and the CPSU. For this reason, Brezhnev and his colleagues tried their best to arrange before the Twenty-Fifth Congress an all-European communist parties' conference which would cope with relations among these parties and the CPSU.[2] But their efforts failed.

As a consequence, the CPSU congress became an open stage for the first revelation to the Soviet public of the deep—and growing—differences and disagreements between Moscow and the most important West European parties. The five thousand Soviet delegates had never heard anything like it before. The third major schism in the international movement (after Yugoslavia and China), potentially at least as significant as the Sino-Soviet rift, was about to take place in Europe—where, many believe, lie Moscow's basic foreign interests.

Enrico Berlinguer, the articulate and outspoken Secretary General of the Italian Communist Party, the largest nonruling party in the world, spoke first. He was an impressive dissident. He demanded not only "open and frank comparison of different experiences and positions" and "equality and respect for the autonomy of each party," as his Rumanian and Yugoslav comrades did, but he also envisaged "new possibilities . . . to advance the dialogue and the convergence between different worker and popular forces . . . including those of Christian inspiration." A useful strategy well-suited to Italian conditions in the troublesome spring of 1976, this was anathema to the Soviet audience. Indeed, Berlinguer argued that "the grave crisis in our country can be solved democratically through social renewal [in cooperation] with forces of different political and ideological persuasion." Berlinguer maintained that "the only socialism possible for Italian society [is] that which will mark the highest stage in the development of all democratic gains, and guarantee all individual and collective freedoms, plus religious freedom, cultural freedom, and freedom for the arts and sciences." For Italy Berlinguer proposed "a socialist society with the contribution of different political forces, organizations, and parties . . . in a pluralistic and democratic system"!

After this bombshell of a speech, the presentation of Gaston Plissonier, the third-ranking member of the French Communist Party's Politburo (Georges Marchais, the French communist leader, like Tito, had decided not to attend the congress), seemed to echo Berlinguer's speech. Plissonier also emphasized democracy, human rights, and freedoms. For the French, he said, democratic socialism "implies a guarantee for all individual and collective freedoms. Naturally, this socialism . . . will assume characteristics specific to our country. It will be a French-style socialism." Plissonier did not mention the recent repudiation by the French Communist Party of the concept of the dictatorship of the proletariat and the adoption of pluralism and democratic, peaceful change as means toward party participation in French politics. Nor did he mention Georges Marchais' criticism of the USSR for violations of human rights and of Moscow's interference in the domestic affairs of other parties. But then, he did not have to. The Soviet leadership, at least, was well informed as to the reasons for Georges Marchais' absence from the congress.

Similarly, Gordon McLennan, the General Secretary of the Communist Party of Great Britain, told the Congress in no uncertain terms that the British party's aim was "the construction of socialism . . . which would guarantee personal freedom, the plurality of political parties, the independence of trade unions, religious freedom, and the freedom of research, cultural, artistic, and scientific activities." Hans Werner, on behalf of the Swedish communists, demanded that "relations among communist parties develop on the basis of equal rights and independence." And Franz Muhri, of the Communist Party of Austria, pleaded for "development of socialism within democracy." And so it went. It may have sounded to some listeners like the beginning of a conspiracy against "proletarian internationalism." It was actually more than that.[3]

On March 1, before the end of the Soviet Party Congress, Brezhnev met with Berlinguer. They were photographed together and issued a joint statement pledging "respect for the independence" of each other's party. But then, after the congress was over, on March 17, Mikhail Suslov in a major address to the Soviet Academy of Sciences, branded as "enemies of Marxism" those who interpret communist ideology in their own fashion: "They slander real socialism, try to wash out the revolutionary essence of Marxist-Leninist teaching, and substitute bourgeois liberalism for Marxism."[4]

What is happening to the West European communist parties? What kind of parties are they? If they are neither revolutionary parties, nor parties of protest, nor parties of reform, what are they? The fact is that fifteen of the twenty-two West European communist parties are electoral, parliamentary parties in search of political responsibility, which actually participate in their national parliaments and in political life at many levels within their countries. The two largest nonruling communist parties in the world—the Italian and the French—owe their success more to political adaptation and ideological compromise than to revolution, reform, or protest. In particular, the Italian party, which has been the leader of this movement toward communist endorsement of responsible, pluralistic, democratic government, not only subscribes to this effort but also prefers collaboration with the Christian Democrats rather than with the Socialists; and it has come around to not only giving full support to the Common Market but to accepting NATO as well.

"Proletarian internationalism," the Soviet international communist strategy—another "dominion [which] cloaked itself in a legitimacy derived from the will of its subjects"—has lost another group of legitimizing supporters.[5] After the schismatics (China and Albania), the independents (such as Yugoslavia and the Communist Parties of Mexico, Iceland, the Netherlands, and Réunion), the neutrals (such as Rumania, Vietnam, North Korea, Laos, and the Communist Party of Malaysia), and the split parties (such as those in Canada, Brazil, Bolivia, Peru, and Paraguay), came the heretics: the major West European parties. They are not willful, just circumstantial; they profit from objective conditions. They have further weakened what was left of Soviet communist stature, authority, standing, and legitimacy. Enrico Berlinguer was stating a fact when he said in East Berlin, after the conference of European Communist Parties in June 1976, that "an international communist body does not exist, and cannot exist, in any form on a European or world level."[6] Proletarian internationalism has failed; communist unity is dead.

It is not only that the West European communist parties have changed and that they can do better if they are more independent and autonomous. Neither is it simply that domestication brings votes and votes bring power. There is also the cumulative effect of Soviet behavior over the years, perceived as oppressive and exploitative deprivation of others, which brings into question the legitimacy of Soviet authority. Has not the CPSU, the socializer of norms, so internalized the relational ties with communist parties that historical changes could no longer cope with the prevailing rigidities? Last but not least, men do seek more than satisfactory and profitable relationships: they seek just ones. And there seems to be a scarcity of just relations between the CPSU and the West European communist parties.

"Proletarian internationalism," then, however important to the Soviet leadership, is no longer the issue. Communism in Western Europe is changing so profoundly that it has less and less in common with Soviet ideology. When Brezhnev declared that "there can be no question of compromise on matters of principle . . . of communist ideology; this is *ruled out* [italics added]," he was speaking to the wind. Those to whom these words were addressed either did not hear, or heard and paid no attention. There no longer seemed to exist a common language among them. Now Moscow would have to yield or else risk a new rift. This may indeed have been the most significant development to emerge from the Twenty-Fifth Party Congress.

chapter nine / *Helmut Sonnenfeldt*

Implications for Soviet-American Relations: Informal Comments

It is a pleasure to be with you at the end of your discussion of the Twenty-Fifth Party Congress. I am actually very interested in what you discussed all day in view of the lack of excitement stimulated by that congress, and I am sorry I missed your discussions: I genuinely would have been interested in finding out what you believe happened there. There has been talk about "Sonnenfeldt doctrines" recently; there is an old Sonnenfeldt doctrine which holds that Soviet Party congresses are more important in retrospect than at the time. I think this congress will probably qualify for that, if it qualifies for anything.

I would like to make some remarks of a general character, putting Soviet-American relations in some perspective. These comments are perhaps fairly basic and possibly simplistic. But I think they are so fundamental to our understanding of the issues before us and to the debate that has been going on in our country recently about the problem of U.S. relations with the Soviet Union that it is important to get some of these basic factors on the table.

The problem that we and the rest of the world face is that the Soviet Union, over the last several years, has emerged as a superpower on a global scale. There have been periods in Russian history when Russia reached out beyond the Eurasian land mass into North America, or within the Eurasian land mass to areas such as India and Iran; or when Russian navies sailed the oceans—not always with rousing success, particularly after the Russians discovered in 1904 that the world *was* round. Now, however, we are in an era when Soviet Russia has, for the first time, and for what looks like an extended period, acquired the attributes of a world power. It has military weapons that have an intercontinental

---

This article is an edited transcript of a tape recording of the author's informal remarks.

reach, and it is only recently that the Russians themselves have understood that these are not merely some new form of artillery that supports land armies, as in the traditional wars in which Russia has been involved on the Eurasian land mass, but are distinct weapons which can be used as the means for influencing behavior at enormous distances from the Russian homeland. That is a novel experience for Russia—one to which the Soviets have been adapting for only a relatively brief period.

There are antecedents to present Russian maritime power in the last century and even the eighteenth century. But the quantitative change that has been occurring in this respect is sufficient to have become qualitative. And here again it is only fairly recently that the Russians have acquired not only the ships and the other wherewithal that makes them a maritime power, but also the techniques and habits of naval power. These proficiencies go far beyond simply having ships; they involve maintaining ships at sea over long periods of time, projecting power at great distances from the homeland, using power on the water to affect events on land. These techniques, which are known to naval powers (and have been known to naval powers for centuries), are relatively novel to Russians.

In other respects, the Soviets have also gradually come only in this generation to define their interests, certainly for the first time in this century and probably for the first time ever, in global terms. Brezhnev had some words to say about that at the Party congress, and there is a phrase that is now fairly standard in speeches on such occasions to the effect that there is no problem anywhere, in any corner of the earth, that can be solved without the participation of the Soviet Union or which does not affect the interests of the Soviet Union.

I distinguish this global perspective from the universalist doctrine that Russians have preached and held for a long time, especially since the Revolution. For while these doctrines were indeed universalist in aspiration and in intent, they were never backed up by the capacity, the power, for implementation in a practical sense. Soviet involvement in the affairs of other countries in the 1920s and 1930s did, of course, occur. The Comintern included many parties at considerable distance from the Soviet Union, and no doubt these parties were largely dominated by the Soviet Union through money and manipulation. But these parties, for the most part, did not control the destinies of the countries in which they operated. They were more part of an international Black Dragon society which had a capacity for subversion and espionage, but which were really in quite a different category of power from the kind of power that the Soviet Union has acquired in recent years.

Now these are perhaps banal and simplistic things to say because they are there for all to see. But there are implications that I don't think we ourselves have fully absorbed as yet.

The first of these is that this entire process is only in an early stage. The growth of Soviet power and its utilization in distant places is a very recent phenomenon, and it is almost certain to continue and become more vigorous in the period ahead. In the life cycle of imperial states, the Soviets must be judged to be in their infancy, not at the end of their lifespan. For us, therefore, the problem of dealing with Soviet power is going to be one of the indefinite future. This realization takes some psychological adjustment on the part of Americans, who are accustomed to dealing with problems in a definitive fashion. We like to solve problems, dispose of them, and go on to the next one. We have done this extraordinarily well in some respects. But our involvement in international affairs, since almost the beginning of our history, or at least since the War of 1812, has been rather episodic. In circumstances where we found we could no longer ignore some external danger, we would apply enormous and overwhelming power, resources, and ingenuity to deal with the problem. In World War I we saw ourselves fighting a war to end all wars, a war to make the world safe for democracy. When we had finished, we decided as a people that it was time to come home and that the problem was solved—at least for some indefinite period of time. Even in World War II, the goal was a definitive solution—unconditional surrender—the ending of a threat, a menace, an abhorrent system on the other side of the fence.

I think that the policy that we developed brilliantly, with extraordinary imagination and energy in the forties to deal with the Soviet problem as it then manifested itself in Europe and on the periphery of the Soviet Union, had a similar goal. This policy, a policy of containment, was one that looked into a fairly near-term future to a time when, after the expansive thrust of Soviet power had been contained, certain internal changes would occur within the Soviet Union that would so transform it as to make it a more normal partner in international relationships and, therefore, in effect solve the problem.

But the problem which we must now comprehend and deal with is of long duration. Like many of the other problems that the United States faces in the world, it is one which is not going to be disposed of in any foreseeable time period. It will have to be managed over a long term, and like numerous economic, political, and other international problems, it is no longer amenable to the traditional American approach of either disengaging ourselves or overwhelming them. Americans thus have to come to terms with the reality that Soviet power is a phenomenon that is here for the long term.

Now the problem of adapting the international system to the emergence of new powers is hardly new. It has existed as long as the international system itself; new actors have appeared on the stage either to join the club, replace existing members, or to disrupt the system. Historically, the process of new actors arriving on the international scene has almost always led sooner or later to the use of force and the outbreak of war. This outcome was brought about because the new actor sought to displace others, through the use of force, and the older actors banded together to ward him off; or conflicts erupted which resulted in the rearrangement of the international system. Yet in the nuclear age, given the consequences of major war, any leader—but particularly American leaders, in the kind of country we are and the values we have—must approach with utmost care and caution the problem that I have outlined: that is, how to cope with both power competition and a system in many respects inimical to our own and to our own values. The recourse to force which has been the traditional response in situations of this kind, while obviously not precluded, is also obviously a course that has to be approached with the utmost sense of responsibility. (The response of force cannot be precluded, because if it were there would be no vital interests—and you can only have vital interests if you are prepared to defend them.) So the problem then becomes that of coping with the emergence of Soviet power, while on the one hand preventing damage to our interests and, on the other, minimizing the danger that this process will result in warfare. Thus we reach the challenge of how to stabilize and limit this competitive relationship.

Now, it is, I think, important to note that, although Soviet power has grown enormously and doubtless is going to continue to grow over the last quarter of this century, this power is extraordinarily uneven. The military power of the Soviet Union is massive and the energies of the country are enormous. Yet the Soviet system itself has substantial weaknesses and vulnerabilities. The Soviet economy has been enormously successful at capital accumulation. It has been far less successful in the process of modernization, in the process of satisfying consumer demand, and in the general process of making the Soviet economy a truly modern economy in the same category as the economies of Western Europe, Japan, and the United States. And it has been clear since the Twenty-Fourth Party Congress that Soviet leaders recognize that *that* process, the process of raising the level of the Soviet economy beyond the stage of a prodigious industrial state to the stage of a modern complex techno-logical society, is going to be very hard to accomplish without some degree of reliance on the external world. Soviet agriculture remains extremely vulnerable to the vicissitudes of climate, and because of its organization and other factors it has remained in many respects the most vulnerable part of the Soviet economy. This has been an element in the Soviet reality that drives the Soviet Union repeatedly to rely on outside contact and support.

Soviet society remains extraordinarily rigid; in fact, it is probably the most rigid industrial society anywhere in the world. It resists innovation. It resists mobility. It is slow to accommodate change. It is weighted down with a hierarchical seniority system that reduces incentives at the lower levels of the ladder and generally makes for a great deal of inertia. In the Soviet system, succession arrangements are still very rudimentary, and it is still not clear whether it will ever be possible for the Soviet Union to produce an orderly succession as leaders come and go.

Furthermore, the whole Soviet empire and the international com-munist movement, which has been part of the Soviet power base, have shown over a period of time extraordinary instabilities. The Soviets have not been markedly skillful at building international structures and inter-national institutions to anything like the extent of what Western nations have accomplished in this respect. Hostilities within the "communist camp" are in some respects today more virulent than hostilities between the communist and the so-called capitalist camp. That certainly has been true of the relationship between the Soviet Union and China. And with respect to Eastern Europe, since that is a matter that has recently drawn some attention, it remains a fact that whatever stability exists in that part of the world rests very largely on the proximity of Soviet power rather than on any kind of structure comparable to the structure that exists, for example, in Western Europe.

I don't want to be diverted now into a discussion of the recent allega-tions concerning my views or the Administration's policies on this general topic; we can return to that when I have finished. The point that

I am trying to make now is that when we look at Soviet power and try to project how it might be used in the world at large, we should remember that the Soviet empire today is not a structure that is comparable to the empires of the past, at least those that were presided over by major European powers, since it is almost totally dependent on the continuous exertion of power and, apart from that, lacks almost completely any sort of structure. The Soviets, in fact, have great difficulty operating in a structure in which power and influence are diffuse. They are very uncomfortable in organizations and institutions which they do not dominate. And when they do dominate a structure, they clearly do not take much account of the particular concerns and impulses within the structure which produce the underlying instability.

Now, as for the Soviet role in more distant places, in Africa, Asia or elsewhere, I think it is well to remember that, first of all, the world in which imperial impulses are played out today is quite different from the world of even thirty or forty years ago, but certainly of sixty or seventy years ago. While still very much subject to manipulation by external great powers, the former colonial world is simply no longer susceptible or receptive to the kind of colonial dominance that marked the empires of the eighteenth and nineteenth and early twentieth centuries. Moreover, the Soviets have not displayed any particular skill at these forms of colonial expansion. They have brought very little in the way of lasting significance to any of the regions in which they have asserted their influence in the last twenty or so years. Their economic and social model has had very little echo anywhere outside the immediate proximity of the Soviet Union, where it has been imposed rather than accepted voluntarily. They have made little contribution to a solution of the problems of development. There is really nothing at all comparable in what the Soviets have done to the British institutions and concepts of public service and justice that the British carried to their colonies over the centuries. There is nothing comparable, at least so far, to French culture and language and law, which the French carried to their colonies in the distant parts of their empire. And even the Germans who plunged into the imperial game relatively late and for a relatively brief period, produced at least physical structures like bridges, highways, schools and hospitals, many of which are still visible today in Tanzania, the Cameroons, Togoland, and Southwest Africa. Anyone who knows anything about Soviet buildings can well recognize that even in this sphere the Soviet contribution has been very sparse. There are some examples, like the Aswan Dam and a stadium here and a structure there, but basically the Russians are not known as the builders of the twentieth century.

So, the Soviet expansion into the world at large has been largely based on power and manipulation, but not on any contributions, at least so far, of lasting value that tie any of these countries positively to the USSR.

I refer to these aspects of Soviet power to stress the point that precisely because there are vulnerabilities in the Soviet system, because there are certain degrees of reliance on the external world, because there are ways in which Soviet society itself can be reached from the outside—a country like ours and the rest of the world can conduct policies whereby we seek to influence and restrain the uses of Soviet power. For that is our basic problem: how can the uses of Soviet power be restrained? How can restraints be built into an inherently competitive relationship?

Basically the policies that have been associated with what used to be known as détente are policies which seek to complement the balancing of Soviet physical power, which is essential and an indispensable task, with drawing the Soviet Union into international relationships that take account of the vulnerabilities and needs of the Soviet system. These are policies which have to do with economic relationships as well as with a whole gamut of relationships in the political, cultural, scientific, and technological areas. Their long-range purpose must be to complement our own capacity to balance—and if necessary, to contest—Soviet power, with our capacity exerted over the long run and in conjunction with other industrialized powers, to draw the Soviet Union into international arrangements which meet some of the real needs of the Soviet Union, needs that stem from those vulnerabilities and weaknesses. By seeking to draw the Soviet Union into this kind of web of interrelationships with the external world, the expectation over the long run is to create incentives for restrained behavior by heightening the awareness that failure of restraint will lead not only to military complications but also place in jeopardy connections which the Soviet Union entered into because of its own needs. That is to say, we seek to establish over a long period of time a calculus of risks and benefits which will operate both in a general and in a specific sense as the Soviets contemplate the uses of their power.

Now, that in summary form has been the purpose of American policy, and the strategy underlying American policy. It is based, to repeat, on a long-term concern with the growth and dangers of Soviet physical power. It cannot expect to deal definitively and conclusively with that problem, but it can hope, over a period of time, to manage the problem in such a way that Soviet power will be externally balanced, that competition will be restrained, and that a war with devastating consequences will be avoided.

You will note from these remarks that I have not attempted to give you a scorecard of who is ahead and who is behind in the game of détente, or to answer the question of who gets more out of détente, of whether it is a one-way street or a two-way street. My point to you is that to focus on those questions alone, even though they may be important, tends to divert us from the prior problem: how to cope successfully with power competition while avoiding nuclear conflict. That is the challenge that is going to be with us for as long as anyone can see ahead. That is an unavoidable problem, and Americans will have to adjust themselves to it. It is in the sense that I have described this policy that I continue to believe that there is no alternative to it. I am not arguing that particular negotiations cannot be conducted differently, that particular issues cannot be stated in a different way. But I would suggest to you that the broad policy approach that I have stated, which involves constructing a balance of risks for the failure of restraint and incentives for its exercise, is a sensible approach; and I would guess that, whatever our other national debates at present, we will have to persist in it.

Appendix:
The Central Committee of the CPSU

TABLE I

OCCUPATION OF CPSU CENTRAL COMMITTEE MEMBERS

	Elected at 24th Congress (1971)		Elected at 25th Congress (1976)	
Party professionals	169	42.7%	179	42.0%
Government employees	144	36.4	163	38.3
Military and security	39	9.8	36	8.5
Other and unknown	44	11.1	48	11.2
Total	396	100%	426	100%

NOTE: Includes both full and candidate members.

TABLE II

SIZE OF CPSU CENTRAL COMMITTEE

Congress	Year	Members	Candidate Members
7th	1918	15	8
10th	1921	25	15
15th	1927	71	50
19th	1952	125	111
20th	1956	133	122
22nd	1961	175	155
23rd	1966	195	165
24th	1971	241	155
25th	1976	287	139

TABLE III

CONTINUITY OF CPSU STATUS

(Percentage of Full Members, CPSU Central Committee
Retained from Preceding Congress CC)

Congress	Percentage Retained
22nd (1961)	49.6
23rd (1966)	79.4
24th (1971)	76.5
25th (1976)	83.4

TABLE IV

FULL MEMBERS OF CPSU CENTRAL COMMITTEE

(by affiliation or role)

CPSU Central organs	14	Supreme Court	1
CPSU secretaries,		Procurator	1
Republic Central Committees	20	People's Control	1
Obkoms, kraikoms, and gorkoms	84	Subtotal	113
CPSU Control Commission	1		
Komsomol	1	Ministry of Defense	13
Trade union council	3	Other military	7
Editors and ideological officials	6	Subtotal	20
Subtotal	129		
		Plant directors	3
Government: USSR ministries, state		Workers and brigade leaders	10
commissions, including planning		Kolkhoz chairman	1
organs and KGB	69	Union of Writers	1
Republic councils of ministers	13	Cosmonaut	1
Presidium, USSR or Republic		Academicians	9
Supreme Soviets	9	Subtotal	25
Ambassadors	14		
Oblast and city executive com-		Total	287
mittee chairmen	5		

NOTES

Chapter One (William Zimmerman)

1. [See, e.g., Leonard Schapiro, *The Communist Party of the Soviet Union* (rev. ed., New York: Random House, 1971); John N. Hazard, *The Soviet System of Government* (5th ed., Chicago: University of Chicago Press, 1971); Merle Fainsod, *How Russia Is Ruled* (rev. ed., Cambridge, Mass.: Harvard University Press, 1963), Part 2, esp. p. 216ff.]

2. See, e.g. Jerry F. Hough, "The Brezhnev Era: The Man and the System," *Problems of Communism*, XXV:2 (March–April 1976), 16–17.

3. [This did not prevent official Soviet commentators from later dwelling on the "contribution of the Twenty-Fifth CPSU Congress to Marxist-Leninist theory." See, e.g., A. Kovalev and A. Kosichev, "Magistral'naia tema nauchnogo kommunizma," *Kommunist* (Moscow), no. 8 (1976). See also Helmut Dehm, "Der ideologische Hintergrund des XXV. Parteitages der KPdSU," Bundesinstitut für ostwisschenschaftliche und internationale Studien (Cologne), *Berichte*, no. 9 (1976).]

4. [See Chapter 8.]

5. *Pravda*, February 27, 1976.

Chapter Two (George W. Breslauer)

1. Andrew McFarland, *Power and Leadership in Pluralist Systems* (Stanford: Stanford University Press, 1969), p. 172.

2. *Pravda*, March 31, 1971, translated in *Current Digest of the Soviet Press* [hereafter cited as *Current Digest*], XXIII, nos. 13–15 (April 20 to May 4, 1971).

3. Alice C. Gorlin, "Industrial Reorganization: The Associations," in U.S. Congress, Joint Economic Committee, *Soviet Economy in a New Perspective* (Washington, D.C.: Government Printing Office, 1976), p. 170.

4. *Pravda*, March 31, 1971, trans. *Current Digest*, XXIII, no. 13, p. 14.

5. *Current Digest, op. cit.*, p. 7.

6. On the industrial reforms, see Gorlin, "Industrial Reorganization"; on the Tenth Five-Year Plan, see Chapter 5 below.

7. *Pravda*, February 25, 1976. Hereafter citations from the speech will not be individually footnoted.

8. *Pravda*, March 2, 1976.

9. [For further discussion of Groups "A" and "B," see Chapter 5.]

10. *Pravda*, March 2, 1976.

[Notes in brackets have been supplied by the editor.]

11. *Pravda*, February 27, 1976.

12. *Pravda*, February 26, 1976.

13. *Pravda*, February 27, 1976.

14. Ibid.

15. Ibid.

16. For some examples, see the speeches by V. V. Grishin and G. V. Romanov (*Pravda*, February 26, 1976); D. R. Rasulov (*Pravda*, February 28, 1976); P. P. Griškavicius and K. S. Demirchian (*Pravda*, February 29, 1976).

17. *Pravda*, February 27, 1976.

18. See Brezhnev's formulation at the Twenty-Fifth Party Congress, and the Central Committee slogans for October 1975 and April 1976 (*Pravda*, October 11, 1975 and April 15, 1976). We should be cautious, however, in interpreting this change, for the intelligentsia is still referred to as the "people's intelligentsia."

19. Darrell P. Hammer, "Brezhnev and the Communist Party," *Soviet Union*, II, no. 1 (1975), p. 10, for a discussion of Romanov's published views on administrative decentralization.

20. See Sidney Ploss, "Coup in the Kremlin?" *The Christian Science Monitor*, November 17, 1971.

21. See Robert Osborn, *The Evolution of Soviet Politics* (Homewood, Ill.: Dorsey, 1974), pp. 431—32, 465—66, for a discussion.

22. See Brezhnev's major speech on the fiftieth anniversary of the formation of the USSR, in *Pravda*, December 22, 1972.

23. For an outline of the discussion among Soviet academics on the problems and prospects for river diversion, see Thane Gustafson, "Transforming Soviet Agriculture: The Party's Gamble on Reclamation" (unpubl., 1976).

24. See the speeches by D. A. Kunaev (*Pravda*, February 26, 1976); S. P. Rashidov (*Pravda*, February 27, 1976); and M. G. Gapurov (*Pravda*, February 28, 1976). While Rashidov and Gapurov called directly for "diversion of part of the flow of Siberian rivers into the Aral Sea Basin and into Central Asia," Kunaev called for "replenishing the rivers that feed the Aral."

25. *Pravda*, March 7, 1976.

26. For summaries of the history of Soviet regional investment policy, see Vsevolod Holubnychy, "Some Economic Aspects of Relations Among the Soviet Republics," in Erich Goldhagen, ed., *Ethnic Minorities in the Soviet Union* (New York: Praeger, 1968), pp. 50—120, especially pp. 86—93; and his "Spatial Efficiency in the Soviet Economy," in V. N. Bandura and Z. L. Melnyk, eds., *The Soviet Economy in Regional Perspective* (New York: Praeger, 1973), pp. 1—44.

27. I base this generalization on a reading of the speeches by all republic Party First Secretaries at each of the three Party congresses during the Brezhnev era. For some highlights of demand articulation at the Twenty-Third Party Congress, see *XXIII s"ezd Kommunisticheskoi Partii Sovetskogo Soiuza* (Moscow: Politizdat, 1966), I, 150, 154—56, 167—69, 178—79, 277—78, 386—89, 420—22,

441–42. For a few examples from the Twenty-Fourth Party Congress, see *XXIV s"ezd Kommunisticheskoi Partii Sovetskogo Soiuza: Stenograficheskii otchet* (Moscow: Politizdat, 1971), I, 150–53, 162–63, 196–97, 212, 445–46.

28. See *XXIII s"ezd*, I, 169, 383.

29. See the speeches by D. A. Kunaev (*Pravda*, February 26, 1976); S. P. Rashidov, G. A. Aliev (*Pravda*, February 27, 1976); T. U. Usubaliev, M. G. Gapurov, and D. R. Rasulov (*Pravda*, February 28, 1976).

30. The contrast between the speeches of Shevardnadze and Aliev at this Party congress is both striking and suggestive. It would be interesting to conduct a comparative analysis of their respective political positions within their republics. Both are natives of their republics and former KGB officials serving as enforcers of Moscow's will against local deviance. Neither has been "soft" on the issue of corruption; but, at least judging by their pronouncements at the Twenty-Fifth Party Congress, they appear to diverge on the broader issues of interethnic relations. The reasons for this divergence may reflect the nature of their local political base rather than their individual personalities—though this is a question to be researched. If it is indeed found to be the case, this would have important theoretical implications for conceptualizing the nature of center-periphery relations in the USSR.

31. At the Twenty-Third Party Congress, the leaders of six republics (Tadzhikistan, Georgia, Latvia, Estonia, Lithuania, and the Ukraine) failed to pay their respects. At the Twenty-Fourth Party Congress, the leaders of seven (Tadzhikistan, Georgia, Latvia, Estonia, the Ukraine, Belorussia, and Moldavia) failed to do so. At the Twenty-Fifth Party Congress, the leaders of four (Estonia, the Ukraine, Belorussia, and Moldavia) failed to acknowledge the special role of the Russian people; this number would be increased to five if we added the double-edged praise offered by Shevardnadze.

Chapter Three (Gail Warshofsky Lapidus)

1. It should be clear that this use of the term, "depoliticization," specifically in the context of intra-elite relations, differs from its more common and imprecise usage in the literature. The term is sometimes used to describe the elimination of political competition, as a systematic characteristic of the Soviet regime, and the imposition of a single political ideology in a one-party system. A second usage points to the removal of the population as a whole from genuine political participation, or more precisely, to the process of "atomization" associated with the Stalin regime. A third usage would imply a reversal of the traditional subordination of all spheres of existence to political direction, a phenomenon more properly described as an extension of the public domain rather than "politicization."

2. For a comprehensive treatment of the problems of systematic social engineering in the 1920s, see Moshe Lewin, *Political Undercurrents in Soviet Economic Debates* (Princeton: Princeton University Press, 1975), and Gregory

Coordination plans of the past usually followed through only to the prototype stage of new products and processes and the issuing of recommendations for series production. As a result, they were often held up for years at the recommendation stage. To remedy this situation, the new programs mandate that items in development be carried through to the manufacture of successful first lots or successful operation of production processes. Not only the manufacture of a new item but also the design and construction of pilot plants and the creation of industrial facilities to be assigned primary responsibility for the manufacture of new articles are specified. The old plans rarely included these measures. See the articles by V. Kirillin in *Izvestiia,* May 15, 1976, and in *Sotsialisticheskaia industriia,* April 9, 1976, and by V. Disson in *Izvestiia,* January 2, 1976.

13. *Pravda,* June 1, 1976. Accordingly, the Academy's research plans for 1976–1980 envisage the implementation and coordination of research on more than five hundred fundamental problems distributed across eighty-four scientific areas. Drafts of thirty-seven long-range comprehensive programs on key problems in the natural and social sciences have also been prepared. An account of this Academy meeting can be found in the *Vestnik Akademii Nauk SSSR,* no. 9 (September, 1976), 3–95.

14. *XXV s"ezd KPSS,* I, 85.

15. See, for example, the speeches by M. G. Gapurov (Turkmen SSR), D. R. Rasulov (Tadzhik SSR), A. E. Voss (Latvia), A. F. Vatchenko (Dnepropetrovsk), A. U. Modogoev (Buriatia), and P. S. Fedirko (Krasnoiarsk).

16. *XXV s"ezd KPSS,* I. 83.

17. Ibid., p. 85.

18. Ibid., p. 164.

19. Ibid., p. 157.

20. *Izvestiia,* May 15, 1976.

21. Brezhnev, *Ob osnovnykh voprosakh,* II, 216–17, 299.

22. *Bakinskii Rabochii,* January 29, 1976.

23. *Turkmenskaia Iskra,* January 24, 1976.

24. *Pravda Ukrainy,* February 11, 1976.

25. *XXV s"ezd KPSS,* I, 328–29. He made the same plea at his own republic's party congress (*Sovetskaia Estoniia,* January 29, 1976), as did Masherov in Belorussia (*Sovetskaia Belorussiia,* February 5, 1976).

26. *XXV s"ezd KPSS,* I, 92, 94.

27. Ibid., pp. 94–95.

28. Ibid., p. 82.

29. This section draws heavily on the ideas discussed by George S. Odiorne, "The Politics of Implementing MBO," *Business Horizons,* XVII:3 (June 1970), 13–21.

30. *XXV s"ezd KPSS,* I, 96, 121.

Chapter Five (Gregory Grossman)

1. "Basic Directions for the Development of the USSR National Economy in 1976–1980" [hereafter cited as "Basic Directions"], originally published in Russian in *Pravda*, March 7, 1976; an earlier but essentially identical version appeared in *Pravda* on December 14, 1975. At the end of October 1976, the Central Committee of the CPSU and the Supreme Soviet confirmed a later version of the Tenth FYP (*Pravda*, October 26–30, 1976), for which no document similar to the "Basic Directions" has yet been published.

In assessing performance during the Ninth FYP period (1971–1975), we shall rely on the following sources: the "Basic Directions"; data on 1975 performance reported by N. K. Baibakov, Chairman of the USSR State Planning Committee, in "On the State Plan for the Development of the USSR National Economy in 1976" [hereafter cited as "1976 Plan"], ibid., December 3, 1975; the report of the Central Statistical Administration on the fulfillment of the 1975 annual plan, in ibid., February 1, 1976; projections by the author from published data (where complete data were not available); and relevant sections of the two major addresses to the congress, those by L. I. Brezhnev (ibid., February 25, 1976) and A. N. Kosygin (ibid., March 2, 1976).

2. Computed from data on annual average employment in Murray Feshbach and Stephen Rapawy, "Soviet Population and Manpower Trends and Policies" [hereafter cited as "Soviet Population"], in U.S. Congress, Joint Economic Committee, *Soviet Economy in a New Perspective* (Washington, D.C.: Government Printing Office, 1976 [hereinafter cited as SENP], Tables 10 and 11, pp. 135–36.

3. See Table 3; and Feshbach and Rapawy, "Soviet Population," Tables 8 and 9, pp. 132–33.

4. See Murray Feshbach, "Soviet Society in Flux: Manpower Management," *Problems of Communism*, November–December 1974, pp. 25–33; and Feshbach and Rapawy, "Soviet Population," Tables 8 and 9.

5. Data for 1966–1970 computed from *Narodnoe khoziaistvo SSSR v 1970 g.* (Moscow: Statistika, 1971), pp. 483, 486; for 1974, *Narodnoe khoziaistvo SSSR v 1974 g.* (Moscow: Statistika, 1975), pp. 526, 528. These figures pertain to the "comprehensive series," which include investment in housing and certain subsidiary facilities of farms and organizations servicing them (see footnotes to cited sources).

6. *SSSR v tsifrakh v 1974 g.* (Moscow: Statistika, 1975), p. 42.

7. See Baibakov, "1976 Plan." This 34 percent figure applies only to fixed investments. It does not include the accumulation of inventories and reserve stocks; nor does it include the very large subsidies on current account borne directly by the budget in the double attempt to stimulate agricultural production and hold down official retail prices. The exact sums of such subsidies in recent years are not precisely known and, in any case, vary widely according to what is comprised within the concept. However, a fairly safe guess is that—as a minimum—such subsidies in 1976 will come to about 20 billion rubles, or over

5 per cent of the expected national income (Soviet series). Nor does the figure in the text include the external outlay on grain and other food imports, which may come to around 5 billion in U.S. dollars in the 1975—1976 crop year.

8. See the contributions of Douglas B. Diamond and the present author, in Norton T. Dodge, ed., *Analysis of the USSR's 24th Party Congress and the 9th Five-Year Plan* (Mechanicsville, Md.: Cremona Foundation, 1971). See also *Soviet Economic Prospects,* cited previously.

9. N. K. Baibakov, ed., *Gosudarstvennyi piatiletnii plan razvitiia narodnogo khoziaistva SSSR na 1971—1975 gody* [hereafter cited as "1971—1975 Plan"] (Moscow: Politizdat, 1972).

10. However, some experts are of the opinion that weather conditions in 1972 were not abnormally adverse; see the account of a conference on the future of Soviet agriculture at the Kennan Institute, Washington D.C., as reported in the *Washington Star,* November 17, 1976, p. A-4.

11. See Table 6 below.

12. *Pravda,* December 19, 1974. The Ninth FYP had set a target of 214 million metric tons. See Baibakov, "1971—1975 Plan."

13. The increase in outstanding medium- and long-term *hard currency* debt in the course of 1975 was about $3.0 billion in U.S. dollars and in the course of 1976—2.7 billion (preliminary). See SENP, Appendix C, p. 738. The Soviet current account deficit in the hard currency balance of payments (excluding gold sales) for 1975 was the equivalent of 6.2 billion in U.S. dollars, according to official Soviet statistics (see SENP, Table 5, p. 732). This import surplus was financed by the aforementioned increase in indebtedness, as well as by sales of gold, arms, and (not least) services.

14. The official assertion (in "Basic Directions") is that the growth in industrial output of 43 per cent (7.4 per cent per annum) just achieved the target laid down in the "Directives" for the Ninth FYP. It does indeed correspond to the lower end of the range stipulated in the "Directives for the Ninth FYP," published in draft form in *Pravda,* February 14, 1971 and, as approved by the Twenty-Fourth CPSU Congress, in ibid., April 11, 1971. However, the final version of the Ninth FYP (*Pravda,* November 27, 1971, and Baibakov, "1971—1975 Plan," p. 345) called for a 47 per cent increase in industrial output. This final version generally narrowed the range of target figures to single figures, typically moving to the upper ends of the ranges. Although the annual plan for 1975 scaled down some targets, the present paper presents all 1975 targets as they appeared in the final version of the Ninth Plan, unless otherwise stated.

15. According to Western calculations, the growth of Soviet gross national product (Western concept) averaged 3.7 or 3.9 per cent over 1971—1975; see Stanley H. Cohn in SENP, Table 2, p. 450, and Rush V. Greenslade, SENP, Table 2, p. 2. Greenslade estimates the average increase of industrial output (though civilian only) at 5.9 per cent per year over the quinquennium; ibid.

16. For natural gas the figure is about 91 per cent.

17. Nevertheless, production of passenger automobiles (which in the Soviet

Union are only partly intended for the domestic consumer) did relatively well at 95 per cent of the target.

18. *Pravda*, February 1, 1976, and "1971–1975 Plan."

19. The index in 1975 was 173 (with the base of 100 in 1970), which just exceeded the target of 172. As indicated in the text, such an attainment is very doubtful. In past quinquennia it has also been common for the machinery and metalworking index to "run away" from the component commodity groups. Since only data on civilian machinery are published, it is quite possible that higher than planned production of munitions may explain the high performance of the overall machinery category. But another very likely reason (given the way the index is compiled) is the much discussed steady, if slow, inflation in machinery prices, which one Soviet source puts at an average rate of some 2 per cent per year (*Sotsialisticheskaia industriia*, July 31, 1975, p. 2), or say, 10 per cent for the five years.

20. *Pravda*, February 1, 1975, and "1971–1975 Plan."

21. An exception was the increase in labor productivity on the railroads, which slightly exceeded its target. This increase seems to have been the result of exceeding the ton-kilometer target by the railroads (which still account for over 60 per cent of all ton-kilometers hauled), which in turn was mostly accounted for by increasing the length of the average haul.

22. Much of the increase in mineral fertilizer capacity came from equipment imported from the West.

23. The choice of the words "Basic Directions" (*Osnovnye Napravleniia*) is an unexplained departure from established practice. On five previous occasions, the corresponding document was entitled "Directives" (*Direktivy*), indicating that the document represented the directives from the Party leaders to the planners regarding the drawing up of the final version of the five-year plan. Perhaps this change in regard to the Tenth FYP is a recognition of the fact that the fundamental directives to the planners are actually given much earlier. (For the slightly revised targets for the Tenth FYP, see *Pravda*, October 26, 28, and 30, 1976.)

24. See our discussion in Dodge, *Analysis of the USSR's 24th Party Congress*, p. 63.

25. *Pravda*, October 18, 1961.

26. *Pravda*, February 25, 1976. The fifteen-year increases work out, respectively, to 6.0 and 4.7 per cent per year on the average. If the category in question is similar to Western-style gross national product, then 6 per cent for 1961–1975 would be regarded as a high estimate by many Western specialists (see Diamond in Dodge, *Analysis of the USSR's 24th Party Congress*, p. 48), while the 4.7 per cent for 1976–1990 may well be regarded as optimistic. Notable, however, is Brezhnev's reference to an economic aggregate including services, which is counter to the traditional Soviet ("Marxist") concept of national income.

27. The figures for 1971–1975 used here are official claims, which in some

cases may be seriously overstated for reasons generally applicable to Soviet official data. Moreover, in some cases they are extrapolations by the author of somewhat earlier statistics.

28. These figures are in rubles; the reported data, therefore, are particularly subject to upward bias because of cost overruns.

29. The absolute production targets for 1980 in energy are: electricity—1,380 billion kwh. (but some 100 billion kwh. for power-station use should be deducted to make the figure internationally comparable); crude oil—640 million metric tons; natural gas—435 billion cubic meters; and coal (all types)—805 million metric tons. Construction of large, multipurpose hydroelectric projects is to be continued, although increased emphasis is to be placed on atomic power in the generation of electricity, especially in European Russia, which is relatively poor in fossil energy sources.

30. The figure in parentheses is our estimate of the official figure for the nonferrous metal industry during 1971–1975. The other figure is computed from the planned average annual rate of increase over 1976–1980 (*Pravda*, October 28, 1976).

31. It should be noted that except where the unit of measure was physical numbers (noted in parentheses), the data represent ruble values. Fulfillment data in terms of ruble value, including our own estimates, are often subject to serious inflation.

32. The official claim in the "Basic Directions" is one of a "4.3-fold" increase during 1971–1975; the planned target was a threefold increase. Thus there would seem to be very large overfulfillment of the Ninth FYP in this respect. However, the index of output of computer equipment and accessories is complicated by likely price inflation and by the collaboration of a number of other CMEA countries in the development and production of the ES ("riad") computer series.

33. From targets for all motor vehicles and for trucks only.

34. See *The Wall Street Journal*, July 8, 1976, p. 1.

35. The sharper drop in investment than in producer-goods output may be occasioned by the high priority enjoyed by defense.

36. See Abram Bergson, "Soviet Economic Perspectives: Toward a New Growth Model," *Problems of Communism*, March–April 1973, pp. 1–9. Since the first version of the present paper was written, Professor Bergson has published an analysis of the Tenth FYP in which he estimates the growth of the (total?) capital stock during 1976–80 to proceed at 6.5 per cent per annum, as against 7.7 per cent during 1971–1975 ("Russia's Economic Planning Shift," *The Wall Street Journal*, May 17, 1976). This estimate of the degree of retardation in the rate of capital formation appears reasonable.

37. The base for the increases is 1975, but these industries apparently have not yet felt much of the effects of last year's natural conditions.

38. Only procurement of eggs and cotton is projected at significantly higher

levels. Egg production has shot up lately, in part thanks to the setting up of large, American-style chicken farms. Cotton was the bright exception in the dismal agricultural picture of 1975.

39. This was the rate of increase of the urban population between January 1, 1970, and January 1, 1976. It is likely to persist for the rest of the decade.

40. See *SSSR v tsifrakh v 1974 g.*, p. 113, and *Pravda*, February 1, 1976. This growth rate is closely corroborated by figures on the retail sale of meat and meat products in the official statistical yearbooks for various years.

41. Kosygin, in *Pravda*, March 2, 1976.

42. The claimed increase during the preceding quinquennium was 42 per cent (ibid.); the impression of what is expected in 1976–1980 is obtained by comparing this figure with the figures for retail sales, incomes, and employment in Table 3.

43. "Basic Directions."

44. *Narodnoe khoziaistvo SSSR v 1973 g.* (Moscow: Statistika, 1974), p. 603; Kosygin, *loc. cit.*

45. Thus, while total agricultural output is to grow by only 14–17 per cent, labor productivity in the socialist sector is expected to increase by 27–30 per cent. By also keeping in mind the demand for manpower in the private sector, one may guess that a 10 per cent reduction of the work force on collective and state farms is foreseen in the Tenth plan.

46. In regard to such measures, see also the authoritative article by N. Drogichinsky, head of the Department of New Methods of Planning and Economic Stimulation of the USSR Gosplan, in *Sotsialisticheskaia industriia*, December 21, 1975. Nearly all measures advanced in this article—and presumably in the economy—are nothing new in principle, but instead emphasize such traditional themes as centralism, amalgamation of production units into larger units, and "iron discipline" in the execution of plans.

47. On Soviet policy toward pricing with regard to innovation, see Joseph S. Berliner, "Flexible Pricing and New Products in the USSR," *Soviet Studies*, October 1975, and my "Price Control, Incentives, and Innovation in the Soviet Union," in Alan A. Abouchar, ed., *The Price Mechanism in the Socialist Economy* (Durham, N.C.: Duke University Press, 1977).

48. Trade with the United States as such is mentioned nowhere in the "Basic Directions." However, the report on the 1976 annual plan did mention the U.S. as one of the seven leading partners among developed capitalist countries from whom the USSR will continue to purchase goods, primarily equipment, on a barter or other basis. See Baibakov, "1976 Plan."

Chapter Seven (Paul Marantz)

1. For another, somewhat different interpretation of the foreign policy implications of Brezhnev's speech, see *Soviet World Outlook*, I:3 (March 15,

1976), pp. 2–11. See also Boris Meissner, "Foreign Politics at the 25th Congress of the CPSU," *Aussenpolitik* (English ed.), no. 2 (1976), pp. 133–52.

2. *Foreign Broadcast Information Service: Soviet Union*, III:44, Supplement 21 (March 4, 1976), p. 12.

3. Ibid.

4. *The New York Times*, January 13, 1976.

5. *The New York Times*, March, 15, 1976.

Chapter Eight (Jan F. Triska)

1. *Pravda*, February 25, 1976.

2. [The long-postponed conference of European communist parties did finally take place on June 29–30, 1976, in East Berlin. For key excerpts from conference speeches and documents, see *The New York Times*, July 1, 1976, and *Current Digest of the Soviet Press*, XXVIII: 26 (July 28, 1976), pp. 1–12. See also *Kommunist* (Moscow), no. 10 (1976), pp. 3–34.]

3. [Key excerpts from the speeches of Berlinguer, Ceausescu, and Plissonier are available in English in *Current Digest of the Soviet Press*, XXVIII:9 (March 31, 1976) and 10 (April 7, 1976).]

4. [For an English translation of Suslov's speech, see *Information Bulletin* of the *World Marxist Review* (Toronto), no. 7 (1976), pp. 44–52.]

5. Werner Jaeger, *Paideia: The Ideals of Greek Culture* (New York: Oxford University Press, 1945), I, 326.

6. Cited in Kevin Devlin, "The International Communist Movement: The Pan-European Conference," Radio Free Europe, Background Report no. 171 (August 5, 1976), p. 13.

Abbreviations and Glossary

apparatchiki	Functionaries of the Party apparatus
CMEA	Council for Mutual Economic Assistance, commonly known as Comecon
CPSU	Communist Party of the Soviet Union
FYP	Five-Year Plan
GNP	Gross National Product
gorkom	City committee (CPSU)
gosplan	State Planning Committee (USSR)
gossnab	State Supply Agency (USSR)
KGB	Russian initials for State Security Committee
kraikom	Territorial committee (CPSU)
obkom	Province committee (CPSU)
oblast'	Province (USSR)
ob"edineniia	Here: production associations
R & D	Research and development
STR	Scientific and technical revolution

Index

Academy of Sciences, USSR, 16, 42–44, 98, 115
Africa, 95, 105
Agriculture, 14–15, 37, 55–63, 66–67, 70–75, 77
Albania, 4, 99
Aleksandrov, A. P., 16, 44
Aliev, G. A., 29, 30, 113
Andropov, Iu. V., 30, 37, 114
Angola, 91, 92
Aral Sea, 112
Arbatov, Georgii, 91
Aswan Dam, 106
Austria, 98
Azerbaidzhan, 23, 48

Baibakov, N. K., 116–18
Baikal-Amur Railroad, 54
Baltic Republics, 22
"Basic Directions," see Five-Year Plan, Tenth
Belgium, 96
Belorussia, 16, 39, 46, 113
Berlin, 99, 121
Berlinguer, Enrico, 97–99, 121
Bolivia, 99
Brazil, 99
Brezhnev, L. I., 2–4, 7–27, 29–52, 55–56, 63, 66–67, 69–70, 75–77, 79, 84, 86, 89–93, 95–99, 101, 112, 114
Britain, 96, 98, 105

Cameroons, 105
Capitalism, 3, 5, 21, 53
Ceausescu, Nicolae, 4–5, 96, 121
Central Asia, 21–23, 25, 44, 112
Chernenko, K. U., 37
Chile, 91
China, 92, 93, 97, 99, 104
CMEA, 76, 119

Communism, international, 32–33, 95–99, 101
Communist Party of the Soviet Union (CPSU): bylaws, 48; cadres, 8, 14, 32, 34–35, 49, 50, 52, composition, 2, 34, 109–10; doctrine and ideology, 1, 3, 8, 10, 22, 26, 40, 42, 99; Central Auditing Commission, 91; Central Committee, 3, 13, 17, 34–36, 37–38, 40, 41, 47–50, 64, 79, 83, 91, 109–10; Politburo, 3–4, 16–17, 19, 35–39, 46, 79, 83, 85, 95, 114; Secretariat, 3, 37; Congresses: history and functions, 1–6; Second, 1; Tenth, 1; Twentieth, 1, 4; Twenty-first, 1, 4; Twenty-second, 40, 114; Twenty-third, 22, 41, 89, 112, 113; Twenty-fourth, 9–11, 22, 24, 26, 41, 52, 89, 93, 95, 104, 113, 117
Constitution, 19
Cuba, 4

Defense, USSR Ministry of, 79, 85, 92
Demichev, P. N., 36
Demirchian, K. S., 112
Détente, 21, 33, 56, 59, 64, 77, 86, 88f, 100–07
Dissent, 40
Dolanc, Stane, 96
Dolgikh, V. I., 37
Donetsk, 7

Eastern Europe, 54, 93
Economy, Soviet, and economic problems, 9–15, 20–22, 41, 43, 47, 52–78
Egypt, 92
Estonia, 49, 113

Far East, 20, 44
Fedirko, P. S,, 115
Five-Year Plan, 2, 43; Seventh
    (1961–65), 60–61; Eighth (1966–
    70), 44, 56, 60–61; Ninth (1971–
    75), 11, 44, 53, 55–62, 64–65,
    67, 70, 72–73, 75, 77, 117; Tenth
    (1976–80), 12, 13, 40, 44, 46, 52–
    78, 93, 116–20
France, 91, 93, 96–98, 105

Gapurov, M. G., 112, 113, 115
Georgia, 17–18, 23, 24, 113
Goldhammer, Herbert, 85
Gosplan, 17, 46, 67
Gossnab, 46
Grechko, A. A., 36, 37, 85
Grishin, V. V., 36, 112
Griškevicius, P. P., 112
Gromyko, A. A., 36, 37, 92

Hough, Jerry F., 3

Iceland, 99
India, 100
Indochina, 92, 93
Intelligentsia, 19, 34
Iran, 100
Israel, 90
Italy, 4, 93, 96–98

Japan, 92, 104
Johnson, Lyndon, 43

Kapitonov, I. V., 37
Katushev, K. F., 37
Kazakhstan, 21, 22
Kebin, I. G., 49
Kennedy, John F., 43
KGB, 18, 37, 113, 114
Khrushchev, N. S., 1, 7, 8, 13, 26,
    27, 29, 31–35, 40, 48, 51, 52, 65,
    66, 84, 86
Kiev, 49
Kirilenko, A. P., 36, 37
Kirillin, V. A., 115
Kosygin, A. N., 9, 15, 16, 20, 27,
    36, 41, 44, 46, 48, 55, 65, 70, 75–
    77

Krasnodar, 16
Kulakov, F. D., 36, 37
Kunaev, D. A., 36, 112, 113

Laos, 99
Latvia, 113
Lenin, V. I., and Leninism, 1, 3, 8,
    11, 14, 23, 26, 30, 37, 51, 52, 89,
    95
Leningrad, 19, 37, 49
"Link" system, 14, 15
Lithuania, 113
L'vov, 47

Malaysia, 99
Marchais, Georges, 97–98
Martov, Iu. O., 1
Masherov, P. M., 16, 36, 39, 46, 115
Mazurov, K. T., 36
McLennan, Gordon, 98
Mexico, 99
Military affairs, 79–88
Modogaev, A. U., 115
Moldavia, 113
Molotov, V. M., 4
Moscow, 17, 18, 23–25, 49
Moslems, 23
Muhri, Franz, 98
Mzhavanadze, V. P., 23

Nationalities, 9, 10, 23–25
NATO, 4, 91, 98
Netherlands, 99
Nomenklatura, 50
North Korea, 99
Novosibirsk, 49

Paraguay, 99
Pel'she, A. Ia, 36
Peru, 99
Plissonier, Gaston, 91, 97, 121
Podgorny, N. V., 36
Poland, 11
Poliansky, Dmitrii, 3
Ponomarev, B. N., 36
Proletarian internationalism, 4, 92,
    95–99
Production associations, 10, 12–13,
    19, 75

Rashidov, S. P., 16, 36, 112, 113
Rasulov, D. R., 112, 113, 115
Réunion, 99
Riabov, Ia. P., 17, 37
Romanov, G. V., 19, 36, 37, 112
Rumania, 4–5, 96–97, 99
Russification, 24–25, 113

Sadat, Anwar, 92
Shcherbitsky, V. V., 36
Shelest, P. E., 37
Shevardnadze, F. A., 17–18, 23–24, 113–14
Siberia, 21, 22, 25, 44, 55, 112
Solomentsev, M. S., 36, 46
Spain, 96
Stalin, I. V., and Stalinism, 1, 23, 20–33, 35, 37, 83–84
State Committee for Science and Technology, USSR, 44, 114–15
Suslov, M. A., 36–37, 95–96, 98, 121
Sverdlovsk, 17, 49
Sweden, 96, 98

Tadzhikistan, 23, 113
Tanzania, 105
Tito, Josip, 96
Togoland, 105

Transcaucasus, 23
Trotsky, L. D., 31
Turkmenia, 21, 22, 49

Ukraine, 22, 37, 49, 113
United States, 33, 40, 53, 57, 58, 89–93, 100–07, 120
USSR, Council of Ministers, 46; Supreme Soviet, 64
Ustinov, D. F., 36–37, 79
Usubaliev, T. U., 113
Uzbek SSR, 16, 21, 22

Vatchenko, A. F., 15
Vietnam, 4, 91, 99
Voronov, G. I., 37
Voss, A. E., 115

Workers' Opposition, 1
World War I, 102
World War II, 26, 57, 102

Yanov, Alexander, 7n
Yugoslavia, 96–97, 99

Zimianin, M. V., 37
Zionism, 90
Zlobin method, 47